# CORRUPTION BY DESIGN: A STUDY OF DESIRE, DEMAND, AND DECAY

PARTHA ROY

ॐ


*In cherished memory of my parents, Late Sachindranath Roy and Late Karabi Roy, whose integrity, compassion, and quiet strength values have continued to inspire me. This book is to their indomitable spirit and the foundation they laid in me. Their names live on through each word I pen.*


ॐ

# Contents

# FOREWORD

Corruption is not simply a crime of law or a failing of ethics—it is a complex blueprint spun into the warp of institutions, cultures, and desires. Corruption disguises itself as need, flourishes in secrecy, and evolves through time and geography. To examine corruption, therefore, is not to merely document abuse, but to question the very structure of authority, the mind of desire, and the deals of ordinary existence.

This novel, Corruption by Design: A Study of Desire, Demand, and Decay, boldly does what many others in its genre never will. It moves beyond veneered stories and reductive descriptions to explore corruption as a thoroughly human condition—systemic as well as intimate, historical as well as new. Within these pages, you'll discover an unflinching analysis of how our cravings, vulnerabilities, and institutions all cooperate to familiarize us with the abnormal on our own unconscious approval.

What is so important about this work is that it refuses to isolate corruption as an outside issue. It asks us to look inward. It asks policymakers, educators, economists, and ordinary citizens to face the unpleasant realities that are hidden behind the rhetoric of reform. It shows us how systems are designed to fail the many while safeguarding the few—how loopholes are not an accident, but intentional.

The writer's recourse to cross-disciplinary thought—from Marx to Rawls, from Ambedkar to Baudrillard—is an intellectual commitment to recognizing corruption as more than a crime, but a social contract turned wrong. The philosophical basis lends the book not only informative, but transformative.

In an age that is full to the brim with anti-corruption rhetoric and performative goodness, what we require is simplicity. Simplicity regarding why reforms consistently collapse. Simplicity regarding the manner in which corruption is maintained by bureaucracy, culture, and class. And above all, simplicity regarding what will be necessary to construct systems that pay back honesty, not fraud.

This book provides that clarity. It calls us to consider: What do we do when morality is turned on its head, when ethics are sacrificed for efficiency, and survival requires complicity? And more importantly, can we turn this tide around?

For anyone who hopes in the possibility of justice, the imperative of institutional change, and the potential of thoughtful citizenship, this book is not a read—it is an reckoning.

# Preface

Corruption is often viewed as a moral failing, a legal aberration, or the fault of a few greedy individuals. But what if corruption is not just an exception—but a reflection? What if it reveals not just cracks in the system, but the system itself? This book is an invitation to explore corruption not merely as an act of wrongdoing, but as a **natural expression of human desire**, shaped by systems, institutions, and economies that often reward it. To understand this argument, we must first journey through time.

### The Birth of Society and Structured Greed

The origins of society were not born out of moral principles but out of necessity. Early human settlements—whether in Mesopotamia's fertile crescent, along the Nile, or the Indus Valley—arose as humans shifted from nomadic tribes to agrarian societies. With agriculture came surplus; with surplus came ownership; and with ownership, hierarchy. The seeds of inequality were sown not as a consequence of evil, but as a function of civilization itself.

As communities grew, so did the need for governance. Chiefs, priests, kings, and scribes emerged not only to manage land, water, and labor but to **control narratives, organize belief systems**, and ensure compliance. **Power was rarely checked**, and more often than not, it found subtle ways to be preserved—through mythology, divine rights, or lineage. What we today call "corruption" often took the form of gifts, favors, or tributes, justified by status and accepted as the norm.

Corruption was not a deviation from order; it was baked into it.

### Empires, Exploitation, and the Mask of Legitimacy

From the Roman Empire to the Mauryan Dynasty, from the Han Empire to the Aztec civilization, we observe a recurring pattern: **centralized control, heavy taxation, exploitative labor, and gatekeeping of resources**. But none of this operated without justification. It was always clothed in the garb of law, custom, or morality.

Rome had its senatorial elites who extracted wealth from provinces while preaching the Pax Romana. China's imperial bureaucracy functioned through Confucian ideals but was riddled with bribery for appointments and favors. The Indian subcontinent, with its caste-coded duties and privileges, institutionalized access and denial under the framework of "dharma."

In each case, **systems designed to maintain order also perpetuated privilege**, and corruption was simply a method of maintaining power under a more palatable name.

### Medieval Morality and the Commerce of Sin

With the fall of empires and the rise of kingdoms and theocracies, **religion became both a moral compass and a political instrument**. The Catholic Church of medieval Europe sold indulgences—pardons for sin—in exchange for wealth. Monarchs extracted rents from the peasantry while granting land and rights to their nobles. In Islamic caliphates, the zakat (almsgiving) system coexisted with corrupt administrative practices. In India, temple economies amassed enormous wealth while untouchability and systemic exclusions thrived under religious sanction.

During these centuries, **corruption took many forms**: the manipulation of faith, the misuse of law, and the commodification of virtue. But it never lost its essential character: a mechanism to **convert desire into control**, and control into reward.

### The Mercantile Age and Colonial Extraction

The dawn of global trade during the 15th and 16th centuries gave birth to a new kind of corruption—**commercial imperialism**. European powers did not just seek to explore; they sought to extract. The Portuguese in Goa, the Dutch in Java, the British in Bengal—all operated under charters, flags, and false pretenses of civilizing missions. Behind these facades was a **carefully designed economic machine that funneled resources from the colonized to the colonizer**.

Corruption became **structural**. The East India Company, for example, was not just a trader but a sovereign power with its own army. Bribes were institutionalized in its operations. Land revenue systems like the Zamindari extracted from the poorest to enrich a foreign empire.

Across Africa, Asia, and Latin America, local elites collaborated with colonial masters, often **selling out their people in return for privileges**. Desire and demand—of spices, land, labor, and later oil and minerals—justified everything from forced labor to genocide.

Colonial corruption was not incidental. It was a **business model**.

### The Modern Nation-State and the Illusion of Reform

The 20th century brought with it revolutions, independence movements, and the birth of the modern nation-state. With it came **constitutions, elections, and institutions of accountability**. On paper, this was the beginning of a new era—where law, not lineage, would govern society.

Yet, paradoxically, **modern democracies provided even more sophisticated ways to disguise corruption**. Electoral funding, political lobbying, bureaucratic discretion, and opaque regulatory frameworks created a perfect storm. Corruption no longer needed to be visible; it became systemic.

The developing world—freshly decolonized—struggled with fragile institutions. In India, the license-permit raj became a breeding ground for rent-seeking behavior. In postcolonial Africa, coups and one-party regimes emerged in the name of national unity, often supported by foreign interests more concerned about minerals than morals.

The Cold War only deepened this rot. Superpowers funded dictatorships as long as they stayed "loyal." In such a world, **morality was expendable and corruption was often geopolitically convenient**.

### The Globalized Age: Legal Corruption and Market Ethics

Today, we live in a world that is more connected and yet more divided than ever. Neoliberalism, privatization, and deregulation have transformed not just economies but also values. Profit is now the highest virtue, and success is measured more by **accumulation**

**than contribution.**

In this world, corruption is often **legal**. Tax havens, lobbying, insider trading, revolving doors between politics and corporations—these are not always punishable under law, but they distort economies and destroy trust. The 2008 financial crisis was a perfect example of what happens when **ethical collapse becomes financially incentivized**.

Even in technology—seen as the harbinger of transparency—corruption takes new forms. Algorithms decide who gets a loan or a job, often reproducing biases. Social media distorts truth in the service of political or commercial gains. In the name of innovation, **we are creating digital monopolies with unchecked power**.

At the same time, the poor continue to pay bribes for basic services—ration cards, school admissions, hospital beds. **There is a corruption of scale for the rich, and a corruption of survival for the poor.**

### Why This Book? Why Now?

In a world increasingly disillusioned with politics, institutions, and morality, this book seeks to ask difficult but necessary questions:

- Is corruption truly a deviation—or a feature—of our social and economic systems?
- Can we separate human desire from acts of exploitation?
- Is it possible to build societies that reward honesty rather than privilege manipulation?

I have not written this book to absolve corruption of its harms. Rather, I have written it to understand **why it endures, why it evolves, and why it feels so natural**, even when we intellectually reject it.

This book brings together **history, economics, psychology, and ethics** to argue that corruption is not an individual pathology but a collective design—born of the very systems we trust to uphold fairness. From ancient empires to modern corporations, from kings to elected leaders, from public officials to private contractors—the story of corruption is not of a few bad apples, but of orchards grown on soil rich with opportunity, power, and unaccounted desire.

As you turn these pages, I invite you not to judge too quickly, nor to seek easy villains. Instead, reflect on the **structures we've inherited, the values we've internalized**, and the choices we make—sometimes silently, sometimes under pressure, and sometimes in denial.

If corruption is by design, then it is also within our power to **redesign our systems**, our cultures, and our conscience.

Let this be a beginning.

— *Partha Roy*

# ACKNOWLEDGEMENTS

The creation of this book has been both a journey of intellectual exploration and personal introspection. While corruption is a topic that usually causes frustration and cynicism, the book was the result of an even greater aspiration—a hope that grasping the origins of collapse can be the initial step in creating a fairer and more ethical society.

Above all else, I give my deepest admiration and gratitude to the memory of my loving parents, Karabi Roy and Sachindranath Roy. Their integrity, humanity, and rock-like faith in the importance of education remain the beacon of inspiration of my life and work. This book, as with everything I have attempted, is a gift to their memory.

To my current and former students, thank you for your unstopping curiosity and willingness to pose tough questions. Your passion gave this project its sense of urgency, and your trust gave it its heart.

I also want to thank the philosophers, reformers, and intellectuals—Indian and international—who have influenced the arguments presented here. From Dr. B.R. Ambedkar, whose vision of justice is still influencing, to Amartya Sen, whose examination of economics, welfare, and ethics informed many discussions here—each was a guiding voice in this intellectual journey.

My gratitude also goes to fellow educators, activists, and public officials who still struggle against corruption not with slogans but with persistent and thankless labor. Their strength reminds us that change is attainable, although the journey may be long and uphill.

I am deeply thankful to my colleagues and friends who read drafts, questioned assumptions, and urged me to continue when the writing was slow. Your feedback honed the sharpness of my arguments, and your support helped bear the burden of this subject.

To the editors, researchers, and designers who saw the relevance of this book and worked to sharpen it into its current form—thank you for your professionalism, patience, and collaboration.

Finally, to the reader: your attention is what turns these pages into action. May this book not only inform, but inspire. May it be a quiet defiance of resignation—and a small addition to a wider collective awakening.

With sincere appreciation,

- **Partha Roy**

# I

# The Nature of Corruption

Corruption is more than a violation of the law or a failure of morals—it is a deep social disease that distorts government, subverts development, and eats away at public trust. To understand its nature, one must peer below surface-level definitions and enter the complex matrix of historical, structural, psychological, and cultural dynamics that support it. As political analyst Robert Klitgaard has put it, corruption can be understood as the equation: $C = M + D - A$, with corruption being equal to monopoly plus discretion minus accountability. This very straightforward equation reflects the underlying dynamics that make corruption possible.

### Defining Corruption: A Multifaceted Phenomenon

The World Bank has defined corruption as "the abuse of public office for private gain." Transparency International broadens this definition to "the abuse of entrusted power for private benefit," thus covering corruption not just in the public sphere but also in business, NGOs, and even civil society. This is necessary because corruption is not limited to government offices; it seeps into day-to-day transactions, from school admissions to hospital services and private contracts.

Sociologist Max Weber cautioned that if unchecked, bureaucracy would become an iron cage of unaccountable power. In those settings, corruption is not just an act, but an institution. It is for this reason that corruption must be understood from a sociological, psychological, and philosophical perspective, rather than a legalistic one.

### Structural and Institutional Roots

Institutions create behavior. If rules are fuzzy, enforcement lax, or punishment slight, then corruption is not merely possible but likely. Nobel laureate Douglass North persuasively contended that institutions are the "rules of the game" within a society. If those rules are hijacked by strong interests, then extralegal arrangements of favoritism and protection prevail over regular mechanisms of fairness and merit.

In most nations, institutional weakness is a colonial legacy. Historian Mahmood Mamdani observes how colonial powers depended on "decentralized despotism"—authorizing local elites to collect taxes and exert control through arbitrary authority. This heritage, never comprehensively eliminated post-independence, continues to inform administrative cultures that prioritize loyalty over legality and obedience over justice.

### Ethical Erosion and Moral Rationalization

Philosopher Hannah Arendt's "banality of evil" explains how normal people get drawn into corrupt systems. When unethical behavior is normalized, people stop questioning it. This is not ideological commitment, but a process of gradual moral disengagement—a psychological process investigated in Albert Bandura's theory of "moral disengagement," which describes how individuals justify unethical behavior by dispersing responsibility or downplaying consequences.

Here, corruption is not merely an exception to norms—it becomes the rule. People justify their own actions as fulfilling survival needs, copying others' behavior, or responding to failures of the system. This dissolving of moral distinctions makes corruption no longer a vice but rather a coping response.

### *Cultural Narratives and Social Conditioning*

Cultural relativism makes it difficult to fight corruption. Anthropologist Clifford Geertz noted that what one society considers corrupt, another will regard as traditional. Habits of gift-giving, loyalty to family, or unofficial negotiation, though culturally entrenched, can turn into corruption where institutional limits are loose. This produces what political scientist Samuel Huntington once called the "moral ambiguity" of modernization, where customary standards conflict with expectations of modern governance.

Furthermore, popular culture glorifies the corrupt—through thousands of movies, books, and TV shows—it sustains the perception that success and virtue cannot coexist. The corrupt are depicted not only as bad guys but as astute survivors, heroes even, who outwit a flawed system. This narrative, told enough, reconfigures public awareness.

### Human Motivations: Fear, Greed, and Necessity

Economist Gary Becker, in his classic work on the economics of crime, contended that people engage in illegal conduct when the expected rewards are greater than the expected costs. Corruption, from this perspective, is a rational decision under limiting conditions. A poorly paid clerk taking bribes might not be devoid of values but of alternative options.

But moral decision is not just an economic one. Psychologists such as Dan Ariely have demonstrated that individuals are likely to cheat a little, enough to gain for themselves but still perceive themselves as good people. This "fudge factor" implies that corruption tends to start with little compromises that grow over time.

### *Invisible Costs: The Slow Poison*

While the immediate financial losses of corruption are astronomical—trillions of dollars a year, says the IMF—the indirect harm is even more insidious. Corruption erodes trust in public institutions, widens inequality, detakes foreign investment, and siphons money away from key services like education, healthcare, and infrastructure.

Amartya Sen, in his book on development as freedom, argued that real development is not merely economic growth but a widening of human capabilities. Corruption undermines these freedoms by depriving individuals of access to equality of opportunity, justice, and dignity The price is not only fiscal—it is human.

Corruption is not only about violating the law—it's about violating the spirit of justice, fairness, and collective development. It's a mirror showing us our ugliest institutional faults and societal hypocrisy. To battle corruption, we need to go beyond punishment and towards change. This means not only changing the laws but redesigning values, rebuilding institutions, and reimagining the purpose of public service.

The journey starts with understanding—and this chapter is merely the beginning. In the chapters ahead, we will discover how corruption gets embedded, how it constructs identities and institutions, and how societies, even the most battered, are able to reclaim their integrity.

## 1.1 Defining Corruption Beyond Law

Most folks who hear the term "corruption" initially think of criminal behavior—bribery, fraud, or embezzlement. It's typically understood as something which occurs when persons violate laws to benefit themselves personally. This holds some truth but merely touches upon what corruption truly is. If we're to understand the complete scope of corruption, we must shift our gaze past the law and recognize it for what it really is: something deeper, something embedded in societies, economies, and even desire.

### *Corruption as a Sign of Societal Disequilibrium*

Corruption is not inherently about violating the law. Corruption is a manifestation of larger issues in a society—issues connected with how power, wealth, and opportunities get shared. Consider this: in cultures where resources are held by a select few, corruption tends to become a lifestyle. For the powerful, it may be a means of holding on to power and preserving their perks. For the marginalized, corruption can be a survival strategy—sometimes, it's the only means of accessing basic necessities such as healthcare, education, or even food.

Here, corruption is not only the result of individual ethical weaknesses, but rather a mirror of fundamental structural disparities in a society. When the system fails to provide an equal opportunity for all, individuals resort to corruption in order to survive, whether in the attempt to preserve their position or get a foothold in the world. It's a cycle: those who have the power use corruption to stay on top, and those who don't have the power use it to survive. It's a self-perpetuating problem.

### Desire and Corruption: A Human Impulse

Now, let's get a bit deeper. Why do people indulge in corrupt practices? It's not always greed or ambition for power. It's human want—our inherent, universal need to feel secure, to be of status, to be acknowledged. These needs can be mighty drivers. We all wish to accomplish something in life, and when proper channels aren't accessible or aren't sufficient, we might resort to corruption as a shortcut to achieve those needs.

Consider: if the system is not allowing you an even break, and you are held back, your aspiration for a better life will make you make choices you otherwise wouldn't have made. It's not a matter of everyone wanting to get rich or find ways around—this is a matter of fundamental human needs. When the standard systems for addressing those needs fail, individuals turn to bribery, manipulation, or other types of corruption to get what they require to survive.

This does not imply that all those who practice corruption are bad or immoral. Most of the time, individuals resort to these activities because they believe there is no other alternative. Corruption becomes a means of satisfying desires that the system ought to have satisfied in the first place. It's an emotional and psychological reaction to a system that leaves individuals with limited alternatives.

### *The Institutions' Role in Corruption*

Human desire, of course, doesn't account for corruption by itself. The institutions—both formal and informal—that shape our societies have a tremendous influence on how corruption occurs. Institutions are the rules we follow, the systems that are supposed to promote fairness, and the structures that govern our behavior. But when those systems fail or weaken, corruption flourishes.

Where the rule of law is poor, corruption is more entrenched. When it is permissible for officials to violate the law without repercussions, it sends a message that corruption is not only okay, but it is essential to make things happen. Think about having to pay a bribe to a government official for basic services. It normalizes itself over time—it's not regarded as an exception, but as the norm.

Likewise, private sector institutions can also propagate corruption. In commerce, with the main concentration usually being profit, ethical practices may at times take a secondary position. This can result in corruption in terms of insider dealing, contract bribery, or other unethical activities geared towards maximizing corporate or individual gains.

And don't forget informal institutions—social norms, relationships, and expectations that shape our behavior. In most societies, behaviors such as favoritism or nepotism are not merely tolerated; they're anticipated. These informal exchange systems serve to perpetuate corruption because individuals view them as being part of the culture. They're not viewed as wrong; they're viewed as necessary to advance.

### *Corruption Around the World: A Global Phenomenon*

Corruption isn't found in just one part of the world—it's a global problem, but it looks different where you are. In some countries, corruption is so widespread that it's just a normal thing. You don't even question it. It's assumed that if you want to get something done, you'll need to bribe somebody or do a favor in exchange. Here, corruption is not regarded as a moral deficiency but rather as a survival mechanism.

Meanwhile, in nations whose institutions are strong and where there is greater likelihood of accountability, corruption is given less lenient views. Nonetheless, even where it is the case, there are corruption existences that remain covert. As much as perhaps it is less tolerated openly, individuals continue to devise ways around the rules. The variance again, once again, is one of institutions, the ones where laws are upheld and individuals brought to account.

We also must take into account the economic structures involved. In capitalist economies, where wealth is typically in the hands of the few, corruption can serve to allow the rich to preserve or expand their dominance. Concurrently, those with less may use corruption to receive access to options that are otherwise unavailable to them. It's a multi-layered, two-way street: the rich employ corruption in order to maintain their grip, and the disadvantaged employ it as a weapon of survival.

### Looking Beyond the Law: A More Holistic View of Corruption

So, what does all of this say about how we understand and fight corruption? If we only see corruption as a breaking of the law, we're not seeing the whole picture. Corruption is more than lawbreaking—it's an expression of deep-seated social, economic, and institutional issues. It's about imbalances of power, unmet needs, and dysfunctional systems.

If we truly wish to combat corruption, then we must do more. We must do more than just penalize those who transgress the law. We must reform the institutions that allow corruption to fester in the first place. That means addressing inequality, building stronger institutions, and fostering environments where individuals are not compelled to become corrupt in order to live. We must remove the causes of corruption and not just be dealing with its effects.

In the following chapter, we will examine the psychological reasons why corruption occurs. We will discuss how the human mind functions in such a manner that corruption can flourish even in cultures where it is deemed to be wrong. By knowing the mental and emotional stimuli that make individuals behave corruptly, we can discover better methods of preventing it from occurring in the first place.

## 1.2 A Glimpse into History: From Democracies to Empires

To comprehend the origin and survival of corruption, one has to explore the roots of governance, society, and the moral philosophies that have shaped human civilizations. Corruption is not a new idea that originated in contemporary political language. It is an old phenomenon, embedded with the aspirations, power dynamics, and institutional arrangements of all societies. Through empires, kingdoms, religious orders, colonial systems, and modern democracies, corruption has accompanied power like a shadow.

### *The Ancient World: Ideals and Realities*

As understood in ancient Greece, corruption was not just about money but also moral and political deterioration. Plato, in his work The Republic, set out the notion of philosopher-king—a leader who would not be motivated by desire, but by wisdom. According to Plato, if the rulers were motivated by their own interests, the political order would necessarily deteriorate. In his celebrated allegory of the cave, he insisted that most humans exist in ignorance, while few are capable of seeing the truth. Governments, then, must be placed in the hands of those uncommon people who have the ability to rise above their wants. Yet even Plato saw the susceptibility of these ideal forms to corruption if rulers became unjust.

His pupil Aristotle further differentiated the forms of government in Politics, specifying six forms—three just (monarchy, aristocracy, polity) and three corrupt (tyranny, oligarchy, democracy). Corruption, in Aristotle's opinion, occurs when rulers rule to their own advantage instead of to the common good. Oligarchy—rule by the rich—is especially vulnerable to corruption, where wealth concentration perverts justice and institutional integrity.

In Rome, corruption was institutionalized as patronage systems, in which offices and favors were traded for loyalty and bribes. Cicero, the Roman statesman and philosopher, cautioned against the perils of moral decay, in which citizens and rulers alike sought personal gain at the expense of civic virtue.

### *Eastern Civilizations and Moral Codes*

In ancient India, works such as the Arthashastra of Kautilya (Chanakya) recognized corruption as a fact of administration. Kautilya, who was a counselor to the Mauryan emperor Chandragupta, wrote at great length about the tendency of officials to abuse power. He categorized forty forms of corruption and suggested rigorous control mechanisms, observing that just as it is impossible to estimate how much water a fish consumes while swimming, it is impossible to identify an official's theft.

Chinese Confucian philosophy also stressed moral rule, with Confucius advocating that rulers become virtuous exemplars themselves. But the Han and Tang dynasties were often bedeviled by venal eunuchs and courtiers. Pre-modern Confucian bureaucracy, though meritocratic in principle through civil service examinations, tended in reality to suffer from nepotism and favoritism.

In these societies, corruption was not necessarily seen as a failure of morality only—it was also a structural issue, due to uneven power, absence of accountability, and centralized authority with minimal citizen scrutiny.

### *Medieval Europe: Power and the Sacred*

In the medieval years, Europe was dominated by church-state entanglements. The Catholic Church, not a religious body, controlled virtually unlimited political and economic power. Corruption within the Church became scandalous, particularly in the sale of indulgences, in the sale and purchase of church offices (simony), and in moral hypocrisy among clergymen.

Martin Luther's 95 Theses in 1517 directly challenged this corruption, starting the Protestant Reformation. He argued that the Church had abandoned spiritual principles and fallen into greed and exploitation. This movement was not only religious but most importantly, political—it revealed how moral corruption could undermine public faith and destabilize the entire system.

Hegel then explored such change in his work using the notion of Geist (Spirit), but pointing out that history moves along by dialectical struggles—conflict and reconciliation among antagonistic forces. Institutions which do not correspond any longer to the ethical spirit of the population then become alienated and must give way to the new structures. Corruption, therefore, serves both as symptom and force in pushing forward the direction of history.

### Colonialism: Institutionalized Exploitation

The emergence of European empires introduced a new form of coordinated corruption—state-sanctioned exploitation of colonized lands. Marx considered colonialism to be the extension of capital's imperative to grow and appropriate surplus value. According to him, capitalism in pursuit of new markets and resources resorted to systemic plunder by presenting itself as civilization.

In India, the British East India Company influenced native rulers, instituted unequal taxation, and sent money back to Britain. Corruption was not a collapse—it was the system. Colonial administrators routinely became wealthy by squeezing bribes and manipulating the economies of native areas. The same trends occurred in Africa, Southeast Asia, and Latin America.

The exploitation was two-layered: economic (looting of natural resources and destruction of native industries) and administrative (corrupt intermediaries, puppet leaders, and coercive legal systems). These systems set the stage for post-independence bureaucracies in which corruption continued as a legacy inherited from colonialism.

### Enlightenment and Early Democratic Thought

The Age of Enlightenment ushered in a new emphasis on reason, freedom, and the social compact. Rousseau, Montesquieu, and Locke contributed to the foundation of contemporary democracy and the principles that power is constrained by legislation and divided between governmental branches. But even within budding democracies, corruption adapted to new forms.

John Locke's political theory of property and consent was most frequently used to legitimate the seizure of lands and colonialism.

Rousseau cautioned in The Social Contract that a democracy could be perverted unless institutions represented the general will of the people.

### Industrial Age: Corruption Goes Corporate

The 18<sup>th</sup> and 19<sup>th</sup> centuries were the periods of industrial capitalism, and along with it, came new ways of political corruption. In America, the Gilded Age became equated with political machines, monopolies, and crony capitalism. Tammany Hall in New York City was the epitome of how politics at the local level could become a patronage and bribery stage.

Karl Marx's attack on capitalism in Das Kapital contended that institutional corruption was not the exception, but a result of the accumulation of capital. The bourgeoisie, holding power over means of production, also controlled legislation, law enforcement, and media, curving public institutions to serve private interests. Marx's base and superstructure theory describes how economic interests condition ideological and legal structures—oftentimes to serve the ruling class.

### 20<sup>th</sup> Century to Present: Reform and Resilience

During the 20<sup>th</sup> century, through the proliferation of democratic values, public accountability as a concept became popular. Anti-corruption agencies, transparency institutions, investigative reporting, and civic action became more robust across much of the globe. With these, however, came new problems.

In modern democracies, corruption usually has more subtle manifestations—through lobbying, regulatory capture, and campaign finance manipulation. John Rawls, in A Theory of Justice, developed the concept of the "original position" and the "veil of ignorance" to design a just society. But in the real world, laws and institutions are often designed by individuals who have a good idea of their own benefit, so Rawls's ideal becomes difficult to achieve.

Global institutions like the World Bank, Transparency International, and the United Nations have all pointed out the ways in which corruption hinders development, consolidates poverty, and sustains conflict. Global attempts to curb corruption, however, tend to conflict with long-standing local systems, cultural mores, and vested interests.

### Corruption as a Mirror of Power

History shows us that corruption is not a fleeting or singular imperfection—it is a symptom of underlying contradictions in relations of power. From Plato to Marx, from the Roman Empire to the internet age, thinkers and systems have grappled with this multifaceted phenomenon. Knowing corruption historically is crucial to engaging with it seriously today.

If we view corruption only as a breach of law, we are overlooking its origins. But if we view it as a socio-political phenomenon conditioned by history, economics, and philosophy, then we start to understand its depth—and our obligation to counter it through vigilance, reform, and moral leadership.

### 1.3 Why We Normalize the Abnormal

Corruption, by its very definition, is the deterioration of integrity—a violation of moral and legal norms. And yet, in nearly every society, what is first seen as aberration tends to creep quietly into acceptance. Why? Why do victims of institutional abuse start defending it, denying it, or even engaging in it? The abnormal becomes normal not because it is desirable, but because it is routine. This process is multifaceted, touching on psychology, history, institutions, and culture.

Let's dissect this disturbing phenomenon.

### The Psychological Terrain: Coping, Conforming, Surviving

Human beings are psychologically conditioned to adjust. When repeatedly faced with unfair realities, particularly when opposition is dangerous or in vain, individuals adjust their expectations. And this is where corruption becomes normalized—not in spectacular scandals, but in mundane choices.

Take, for instance, the office worker who bribes his way to have his pension documents approved, or the student who offers a bribe to the professor in anticipation of mercy. At first, these actions feel wrong. But when everybody else is doing it, when it seems to be the only way to proceed, the brain starts to justify. "It's just how the system works." "I have no choice." This is cognitive dissonance in action—alleviating the tension between one's values and actual experiences by changing perception instead of challenging the system. With time, the unthinkable becomes ordinary.

### *Cultural Narratives: From Tolerance to Celebration*

Culture doesn't simply mirror society—it molds it. And in most cultures, the seeds of normalizing are planted early on. Acts such as nepotism or "greasing the palm" can be theoretically disapproved of, but are usually shrouded in traditions of family responsibility or deference to authority.

In some parts of the world, bribing is compared to paying a tip. For others, cheating the system for self-interest is viewed as cunning, not crime. Folklore, street humor, and religious dogma can subtly legitimize rule-bending if it benefits one's family or clan. The cunning trickster who tricks the mighty is a champion character in many oral traditions. When such conduct is lionized instead of criticized, right and wrong become confused.

### *Institutional Frameworks: Constructed on Faulty Foundations*

Most institutions around the globe are not just victims of corruption—call them enablers. Bureaucracies created without checks in place to ensure transparency turn into impenetrable fortresses. Judicial systems with weak independence or enforcement capabilities cultivate impunity. Patronage-based political parties, which reward loyalty above merit, cultivate both.

The longer such imperfect systems exist, the deeper corruption becomes ingrained in the "rules of the game." Good people conform or are driven out. Merit-based promotion becomes the exception. Systemic failure is eventually confused with natural order over time.

And worst of all, when someone does stand up—whistleblowers, journalists, or reformist leaders—they get punished or silenced, confirming that fighting corruption is risky, even stupid.

The Economic Reality: Inequality as Fuel

Desperation and inequality are potent grease for corruption. Where employment is scarce and salaries low, corruption is used as a means of oppression and survival. A traffic officer underpaid might accept bribes not from greed, but because it augments an unsustainable wage. On the other hand, a successful contractor might bribe officials to circumvent safety protocols, thinking it's just another business expense.

This interdependence—the corrupt public servant and the desperate citizen— produces a cycle of normalization. When public services are unstable, citizens resort to shortcuts. These shortcuts commonly include informal payments or connections. Over time, the notion of fairness is diluted, and the public no longer expects anything more.

***Historical Continuity: Colonialism, Feudalism, and Inherited Corruption***

Corruption does not occur in isolation—it is bequeathed and evolved over the centuries. The colonial powers commonly operated exploitative bureaucracies, employing divide-and-rule measures, nepotism, and faithful intermediaries to manage the masses. The systems rewarded collusion, frequently at the cost of integrity.

Even post-independence, most post-colonial countries still had the administrative framework of their colonizers. The language shifted, but the framework stayed the same. What was once the imperial taxman turned into the new bureaucrat—still holding absolute power over common folks. As Marx would see it, history tends to repeat itself—first as tragedy, then as farce. The tragedy of colonial exploitation spawned the farce of post-colonial misgovernance, veneered with nationalist propaganda.

Likewise, Hegel's dialectic reminds us that systems of history develop through struggle—but not necessarily toward the better. In much of the world, feudal patronage systems merely evolved to meet the requirements of modern democracy. Voters were clients, politicians were patrons, and the vote was a transaction.

***Philosophical Framing: What is "Normal"?***

Philosophers like Plato believed that a just society must be guided by reason, not appetite or ambition. Yet in the real world, it is often base instincts—greed, fear, pride—that dominate governance.

The dissonance between Plato's "philosopher king" and the modern corrupt politician is a testament to how far society has drifted from the ideals of governance.

John Rawls, in his justice theory, invites us to envision society from behind a "veil of ignorance"—having no idea what our position in it will be. If individuals planned society with no idea if they would be rich or poor, powerful or powerless, they would insist on fairness. Corruption is the victory of certainty over justice: the powerful know they will gain and therefore plan institutions to secure themselves.

### *Media and Pop Culture: The Double-Edged Sword*

The media of today has great power in determining what is normal to people. Investigative journalism exposes corruption on one side. On the other, movies and television shows tend to glamorize it. The corrupt policeman, the dishonest businessman, the cunning politician—they're shown with charm and swagger. When the villain is made a hero, or when corruption is trivialized as entertainment, the moral compass of the public loses its magnetic north.

Baudrillard's "hyperreality" comes to mind here. When citizens are assaulted with images of reform and change—fake audits, pretend arrests, empty speeches—they start mixing performance with reality. Spectacle becomes more important than substance. People cease demanding true reform because they're given the illusion of it.

### *The Global Perspective: A Common Malady*

Normalization of corruption is not unique to any one country or culture. From corporate lobbying scandals in the West to petty bribery in the Global South, corruption wears many masks. In developed countries, it is often sanitized through legal loopholes, lobbying, and revolving doors between government and industry. In developing nations, it tends to be more overt and transactional.

But the psychology is the same: when unethical practice is profitable, goes unpunished, or even rewarded, it becomes the norm.

### *The Way Forward*

In order to denormalize corruption, we need first to acknowledge its normalization. That is not straightforward. It calls for moral courage, historical knowledge, and institutional integrity. Education should encourage critical thinking, not blind conformity. Governance should make transparency a higher priority than theatrics. Citizens need to reassert their power—not only at the ballot box, but in ordinary decisions.

Normalization is not destiny—it is design. And what is designed can be redesigned. It starts with a question: What kind of society do we want to live in?

### 1.4 The Moral Paradox: When Right Feels Wrong and Vice Versa

A very serious tragedy in any corruption-ridden society is not the commonality of immoral acts per se, but the insidious and incremental breakdown of our general moral compass. Corruption has, over time, the evil capability to reverse the moral order. What starts out as disquiet at wrongdoing quickly evolves into passive acceptance, followed by normalization, and ultimately admiration of the cunning of the wrongdoer. This is where a society descends into a perilous moral contradiction, in which doing what is right is wrong—or worse, pointless—and doing what is wrong is smart, practical, or even necessary to stay alive.

This inversion of morality does not occur suddenly. It is the cumulative result of years of disappointment, failed institutions, broken promises, and unfaced injustices. People start by compromising "just this once" for what they think is a practical requirement—maybe paying a bribe to expedite a service or secure their child an entry into a good school. But over time, this "exception" turns into the rule. Individuals begin believing that the system itself cannot operate in the absence of these moral shortcuts, and that those who won't play along are not merely naïve, but self-destructive.

This paradox is particularly perilous because it makes morality itself a liability. Honesty, rather than being rewarded, becomes a liability. A honest officer can herself be ostracized, denied promotion, or harassed. A teacher who refuses to pad marks may be punished for being "rigid" instead of commended for integrity. A student who declines to cheat may find themselves derided by classmates and sanctioned by a system that doesn't value merit at its purest. And when these instances pile up and go unpunished, youth—whose developing minds are still forming a sense of justice—grow up confused, conflicted, and cynical.

In corrupt systems, this moral paradox is not only an unfortunate side effect but an actively supported framework. The reward system is askew. The rules are enforced selectively. The gatekeepers of accountability are too often themselves tainted. And this results in what one might call an "ethics penalty" – where doing the right thing is more costly than doing the wrong. In psychological terms, this results in what scholars describe as ethical dissonance. People bear the weight of knowing they are right but unable to act on it for fear of social, professional, or economic consequences.

These inconsistencies do not stay within the individual level. They infect the cultural conscience. When movies, the media, and even schoolbooks just keep going on about being moral while society as a whole only rewards intelligence and deception, humans start living two moral realities. In one, they hold in their minds honesty, goodness, and fairness as ideals. In the other, they manage by means that negate those ideals. This contradiction gives rise to fatigue of the soul. People start giving up bit by bit. Not because they want to but because they feel that integrity can no longer hold a place within their everyday world.

Look at how children get raised seeing parents live life. A father who tells his son to be honest also bribes the official in the municipal building to get the certificate. A mom who educates her daughter on fairness can also employ influence to cut in front of a waiting list for entry. The message is one of clarity: the moral codes we are talking about are virtuous but not necessarily humanly possible. Children start internalizing that justice and truth are not ideals to maintain but ideals to dream about—noble, certainly, but unrealistic in "the real world." In doing so, the paradox is perpetuated from generation to generation, not merely as a thought but as an adaptation.

The psychological cost of this reversal is severe. Individuals who used to hold beliefs about change and progress fall back on apathy. Idealism gives way to skepticism. The distinction between right and wrong starts to dissolve until the language of ethics is drained of any meaning. If a young bureaucracy member enters government service with fervor but later discovers that chances for advancement lie more in displaying loyalty to immediate superiors rather than to serving the public, they not only lose motivation but also faith in the very ideal of duty. When a small businessman comes to the realization that success hinges on the number of hands he greases and not the quality of his work, he internalizes that competence is secondary to contacts. These disillusionments, as individual, lead to a mass moral numbness.

Even the media, who are supposed to be the moral mirror of society, at times play into this paradox. Hollywood films and web series often romanticize the "clever criminal" or the corrupt official who beats the system. These are not villains, but heroes of a flawed system. The message, unwittingly or otherwise, is that success is not for the honest, but for the brazen. Such portrayals reinforce a deep-seated belief among ordinary people: that in a corrupt world, honesty is a disadvantage unless it is strategic.

Philosophers have warned us of this danger for centuries. Plato's allegory of the Ring of Gyges raises the haunting question: would anyone act justly if they could escape consequences? In societies where laws are inconsistently applied and accountability is rare, many indeed act as if they wear such a ring. Meanwhile, those who refuse to wear it often suffer in silence, isolated by a society that mistakes compromise for wisdom and silence for maturity.

The biggest loss, though, is not material—moral. When individuals give up believing goodness counts, honesty counts, and justice is real, the heart of society becomes endangered. We lose our ability to envision a better world. Corruption, in that sense, is not only a violation against governance—it's a theft of shared hope. It destroys our moral imagination, making us forget what it is like to live in a society where right feels right and wrong feels wrong.

The answer, therefore, cannot lie in punitive laws alone. We need a cultural and educational rebirth—one that recaptures the nobility of ethical conduct and reasserts moral simplicity in our homes, classrooms, and public conversation. Integrity must be made pay, both in material goods and social regard. Truthful officials should not only be shielded but also hailed publicly. Moral teachers, physicians, reporters, and civil servants should be raised up as models—not only in textbooks, but in ordinary talk. Our children should not only hear about moral values, but see them practiced.

Only then can we hope to turn this paradox around—only then can we guarantee that the next generation will not grow up in a world where right is wrong and wrong is right. Only then can we restore the soul of our society and point the compass of our nation toward justice, empathy, and truth.

## 1.5 Corruption in Daily Life: Micro-Level Deviations

Corruption has usually been conceived as a large-scale phenomenon, one which is connected to top politicians, multinational corporations, or corrupt government officials who are involved in embezzling public funds. Yet the truth about corruption is much broader than this prevalent and visible scale of malfeasance. Corruption permeates daily life, in seemingly petty and insignificant interactions that define our daily reality. These micro-level violations, though most times reduced to mere trivialities, are the building blocks of a much larger systemic problem. When added together over time, these minor corrupt acts weaken the social fabric, reinforcing the idea that corruption is not only necessary but also an inevitable part of living.

### *The Subtlety of Everyday Corruption*

In contrast to the open and sensational corruption that tends to grab the headlines, ordinary corruption takes place in the hidden realms of everyday encounter. It can be observed in a public official who accepts a bribe to hurry up a normal service, a teacher in school who expects gifts for improved grades, or a traffic policeman who allows a car to pass through in return for a small "tip." These minute deviations usually escape attention or are deemed too inconsequential to oppose, but they do no less harm to the honor of the system.

The inclination to ignore these minor acts of corruption is connected to what social scientists call "moral licensing." Basically, when we perform a small wrong, we excuse ourselves for it because it doesn't appear to result in great harm. The bribe demanded by the clerk isn't as much of a concern as the corrupt transactions of a high official. Both, however, are responsible for normalizing corrupt actions.

This micro-level normalization of corruption is what contributes to the wider societal embrace of unscrupulous practice. The little bribe to navigate a bureaucratic procedure or bending the rules to advance becomes the unspoken component of the system, rooted in the norms for how business is "done." Years later, these practices are transmitted as learned behavior, creating norms for subsequent generations. What was a rare exception soon becomes part of the system.

### The Individual's Role in Perpetuating Corruption

At the individual level, choosing to commit these micro-corruption acts is often done after rationalization. The individual who accepts a bribe or gives a bribe to advance may rationalize their actions as a necessary means to survive or as a way to navigate an inefficient system. The logic is simple: "Everyone is doing it," or "This is how the system works." In environments where inefficiencies are pervasive, where laws are inconsistently enforced, and where public services are slow and unresponsive, individuals begin to see corruption not as a deviation but as an essential strategy to achieve their goals.

This mentality is particularly common in societies where formal channels of justice and accountability are weak. Individuals soon discover that pure merit is generally insufficient to flourish in such schemes. Rather, they are rewarded for using their personal connections, influence, and even illicit behavior. A pupil, for example, may pay a teacher to pass an exam, believing the "rules" of the academic system are not in their favor. Likewise, a candidate may be forced to pay an unauthorized fee for an interview opportunity or to hasten the recruitment process, convinced that their qualifications are not enough in a situation where widespread nepotism exists.

With time, this dependence on corrupt methods, even in matters that appear insignificant, becomes part of the culture. It is not viewed anymore as an immoral action but as something that has to be done. And when individuals get used to such a perception, they tend to carry this act to other areas of life and solidify the corrupt system even more.

### *Cultural Acceptance and the Role of Social Norms*

The acceptance of micro-level corruption is also strong culturally. In most societies, what may amount to corruption in one situation becomes a type of social obligation somewhere else. Such is particularly prevalent in cultures wherein gift-giving, reciprocity, and acquaintance are very much part of ordinary life. Public officials in certain areas, for instance, get gifts or favors from some parties not as aberrations but rather as expected acts. Although such behavior could be technically classified as bribery, it can often be excused or even justified on the grounds of ensuring social harmony and building personalized relationships.

In such societies, the line between ethical conduct and acceptable conduct gets effaced. This is easy to observe in most countries where it is common-place to pay doctors, teachers, or bureaucrats on a casual basis. The concept of fairness and equity is undermined, and an individual's success or resource access is based not on merit or need but on willingness to participate in such informal schemes.

Normalization of corruption on a micro-scale also contributes to the influence on public perception. When people are repeatedly exposed to such activities on a daily basis, they end up being numb to the damage that corruption inflicts on society. They witness their peers taking part in petty acts of corruption without consequences and conclude that it is not just normal but natural.

### Economic Pressures and the Survival Instinct

In poor countries or in situations where unemployment and poverty are widespread, micro-level corruption tends to become a survival strategy. Government officials, whose salaries are not enough to cover their basic needs, might ask for bribes to survive. A clerk might perceive accepting small bribes as the only means of supporting their family. Likewise, low-income students may bribe their way into universities to get opportunities that they feel are otherwise out of their reach.

In these settings, corruption is a rational option—one that is not greed-related but necessity-based. It is an avenue of compensating for the insufficiency of proper public services or economic opportunities. The underlying economic imperatives make it so that corruption is not only commonplace but institutionalized as a means of survival. The moral framework shifts as people place their material needs and survival above ethical rationality.

Additionally, the absence of accountability and transparency in these mechanisms worsens the situation. Individuals perceive that there is little to no possibility of being held accountable for minor corruption acts. Without proper enforcement mechanisms, such practices become habitual. This promotes a vicious circle, wherein lack of accountability leads to more corruption, which further destroys the institutions responsible for implementing the rule of law.

### The Long-Term Effect on Society

The micro-level deviations of corruption, although commonly regarded as trivial or irrelevant, bear immense long-term implications. The minute daily actions of corruption, collectively considered, result in a culture of mistrust and inefficiency. Corruption normalizes the undermining of public trust in the institutions responsible for public welfare. Citizens who frequently participate in or observe corrupt practices start losing their belief in the equitability of the system, thinking that their own success will be determined by whether they can manipulate or bribe their way through the system instead of talent and effort.

In addition, continued sustenance of these micro-level corrupt practices retards economic and social progress. Funds meant for public services are diverted by way of bribes and other unlawful means. This denies the public basic services like healthcare, education, and infrastructure, thereby promoting more inequality and social instability in the long run. Eventually, corruption at all levels in society becomes automatic and corruption is perceived as normal, while morality becomes an exception.

Overall, micro-level corruption deviations are not as small as they would seem at first glance. These small actions, when done time and again in society at large, amount to a normalization of corruption and reinforce a culture of untruthfulness and selfishness. The cycle must be broken through a collective effort at challenging and remaking the very systems and norms that render corruption the sole workable option for survival. By means of education, responsibility, and a desire for transparency, societies are able to start right at the root of corruption—beginning with the micro-level departures that govern daily life.

# II

# Desire and Demand – The Seeds of Corruption

Corruption is often perceived as an individual moral failing or a systemic lapse, but its roots go deeper into the fertile soil of human desire and societal demand. It is not born of darkness alone; it emerges from the interplay between aspirations and obstacles, between what people long for and what society allows them to attain. The story of corruption, therefore, is inseparable from the story of our wants and our needs—especially when these wants are inflamed by inequality, insecurity, and the craving for recognition.

From early childhood, individuals are exposed to models of success that are rooted less in character and more in possession. Societies saturated with consumerist ideals condition people to believe that value lies in the things they own, the status they display, and the privileges they can access. The humble desire for a better life—when thwarted by systemic barriers—morphs into a more dangerous form of entitlement. In this environment, corruption often begins not as a deliberate crime, but as a small act of desperation, a compromise made to survive, to fit in, or to rise up.

What begins as a harmless shortcut can soon become a habit. The schoolchild who sees a peer get ahead by dishonest means, the jobseeker who learns that success depends on 'knowing hope right person', or the underpaid official who sees bribery as the only way to sustain a dignified life—each becomes a participant in a much larger economy of corruption. This is not merely a moral failing; it is a social contagion that spreads when fairness is scarce and pressure to succeed is overwhelming.

The modern world intensifies this pressure. Globalization has not only connected markets, but also connected dreams. Social media and mass advertising expose people to lifestyles that are often unattainable through honest means, especially in regions where social mobility is limited and economic disparity stark. In such a world, desire is no longer guided by need but by comparison. A person is measured not by their intrinsic worth, but by how closely they mirror the glamorous images they see around them. And when the means to reach that ideal life are inaccessible, corruption provides a way in—a risky but sometimes rewarding path to inclusion.

This is where demand comes in—not just economic demand, but social and psychological. When millions of students compete for a few seats in a prestigious college, when thousands fight for one government job, or when resources are limited but expectations are endless, the demand for privilege fuels the black market of influence. The system itself begins to cater to this demand. Brokers emerge, loopholes are exploited, and power becomes commodified. Corruption becomes a parallel mechanism through which access is negotiated—not legally, but transactionally.

At its core, this system of corruption mimics the logic of a marketplace. Scarcity drives value; opportunity becomes a product; and ethics are sidelined for efficiency. People begin to pay for what they deserve to receive freely—justice, education, jobs, permits—and in doing so, they unknowingly legitimize an illegitimate structure. Over time, even those who abhor corruption become complicit, simply because the alternative seems hopelessly slow, uncertain, or non-functional.

But it is not just material desperation that drives corruption. Sometimes, it is ambition. Those who already have enough still crave more—more recognition, more influence, more visibility. In their minds, playing by the rules seems inefficient or naive. They believe the system itself is a game, and those who succeed are the ones who know how to play it better—not with effort, but with manipulation. This perception distorts public morality. When the rich get richer through connections, when the powerful evade accountability, the message that trickles down is dangerous: that honesty is a handicap.

The tragedy lies in the moral confusion this generates. Society sends mixed signals. It teaches children to be honest, yet rewards those who bend the rules. It glorifies clean hands, but idolizes flashy success, regardless of how it is attained. People begin to feel foolish for following the law, and clever for breaking it without getting caught. This inversion of values hollows out the moral fabric of communities. The honest begin to feel like outcasts. The corrupt become role models.

Moreover, corruption does not always wear a villain's face. It often appears as compromise, as adjustment, as 'just the way things work here'. In many societies, small acts of corruption—like bribing for a license, faking a certificate, pulling strings for admission—are so normalized that they cease to shock. They are viewed not as crimes, but as tactics. This normalization is dangerous because it turns systemic failure into personal adaptation, thereby erasing the urgency for reform.

Yet, blaming the individual is not enough. To truly understand corruption, we must understand the context that enables it. When institutions are weak, procedures opaque, and enforcement arbitrary, people lose faith in the system. They begin to believe that fairness is a myth and that only those who maneuver or manipulate can survive. In such a landscape, desire becomes distorted and demand becomes corrupted. Education, health, law, governance—nothing remains untouched.

And yet, hope is not lost. Human beings are capable of not only dreaming but also of imagining better systems. To tackle corruption, we must not only punish the guilty but also reduce the incentives that make corruption profitable. We must build institutions that function with integrity, fairness, and transparency. We must replace symbols of excess with stories of dignity. Above all, we must rewrite the narrative of success—not as something to be seized at any cost, but as something to be earned, together, within the bounds of justice.

Desire and demand are essential to human progress. But when they are shaped by fear, inequality, and insecurity, they turn into the seeds of corruption. To weed out those seeds, we must water the roots of equity, access, and accountability. Only then can we nurture a society where ambition is not suppressed, but where it is fulfilled with honor.

## 2.1 Human Wants: From Necessity to Surplus

Human wants are as old as humanity. In their most primitive manifestation, they start with the essentials—food, water, shelter, protection. These are not decisions but necessities, the biological and climatic requirements of staying alive. Through history and across geography, the first civilizations organized their social lives and economies with the aim of supplying these fundamental necessities. But human wants are not fixed. Once survival is guaranteed, a second, more sophisticated desire appears—a desire for comfort, for status, for identity, for meaning.

This move from need to want, and from want to excess, is not simply an economic path but a deeply psychological and philosophical one. As the 19$^{th}$-century economist Alfred Marshall rightly pointed out, "Wants and their satisfaction are the basis of all economic activity." The moment a person secures their survival, their desires evolve and expand. What was once luxury becomes necessity. The thatched hut becomes a concrete house; the bicycle gives way to the car; simple meals are no longer sufficient, and branded lifestyles take over. This process—often referred to as the "hedonic treadmill"—demonstrates the way in which human beings continually reset their aspirations higher, but seldom achieve any lasting satisfaction.

In contemporary cultures, this cycle is fueled by exposure. Via mass media, advertising, and social media today, not only are people informed of what they do not have, but they are reminded on an ongoing basis how somebody else does. Comparison is an obsession. A village farmer once satisfied with his harvest now looks at videos of technology businesspeople in glass skyscrapers. A child from a middle-class background sees influencers parading designer fashion and foreign holidays. The yearning that was constrained by geography and class now sees no bounds—only screens connecting all people and yet, strangely, segregating more than it brings together.

This shift of want—from natural to manufactured—is what gives rise to corruption at micro and macro levels. When an individual feels left behind or ignored, not due to lack of effort but due to lack of access, the urge to circumvent the system arises. The want itself is perhaps not immoral—everyone desires a good life—but the avenues open to fulfill it seem shut or unjust. This disconnect between desire and possibility breeds what development economist Amartya Sen refers to as "capability deprivation": the loss of one's actual freedom to live the type of life one cares about.

The problem is not with desiring more, but with desiring more in a world that offers everything but delivers selectively. When individuals realize that merit is no guarantee of success—that connections, influence, or manipulation are more important—their desires get skewed. The path from survival to excess is one tainted by moral compromise. The unemployed graduate who pays for a job, the businessman who cooks books to avoid tax, or the student who uses a forged certificate to gain admission to college—they are not necessarily born cheaters. Occasionally, they are simply burned out by a system that refuses to reward patience or principle.

More dangerously, the normalization of over-want undermines the boundary between ethical ambition and unethical greed. It is taken for granted that in order to "get ahead," one must "do what it takes." The line between need and greed is erased, as individuals pursue possessions not to enhance their lives but to surpass others. In this competition for prestige, more becomes the standard of value, and virtue is secondary. The issue is not that individuals desire more; the issue is that society leads them to want more without pause.

Even the most vulnerable are not immune. A slum dweller will accept a bribe to allow illegal water connections to function—not out of evil, but because they watch others benefitting as they continue to struggle on a day-to-day basis. A teacher might leak exam papers not because they lack ethics, but because they watch the education system simplified into competitiveness and disorder. At every level, wants balloon under pressure. What starts as a human impulse ends up being systemic distortion.

In order to combat corruption, therefore, we need to begin by knowing how human desires develop—and how they are fashioned not just by real need, but by manufactured scarcity, by insecurity, and by inequality. Education has an important part to play in this. It can be the mirror that enables people to see the distinction between progress and pretence, between achievement and accumulation. It can root people in values that curb excess desires and favour collective good over individual benefit.

In the end, human desires are not to be feared. They are the driving force for progress, for progress, for exploration. But when values are separated from wants, and excess is idealized while integrity takes a backseat, the same engine can drive society into a spiral of greed and shame. Power may plant the seeds of corruption—desire sows them in fertile soil. In order to construct a fair and equitable world, we have to begin not only with laws or institutions, but with the internal compass of human desire. And that compass has to be guided by empathy, justice, and wisdom.

## 2.2 Greed, Fear, and Insecurity as the Drivers

Corruption seldom manifests in isolation. It is an outcome of behavior deeply ingrained in the emotional environment of human existence. Of the most significant psychological drivers of corrupt behavior are greed, fear, and insecurity. These three drivers—albeit distinct in themselves—frequently overlap and feed off one another, building an overwhelming momentum toward moral compromise.

Greed is the most public of the three, and perhaps most socially accepted. In an ever-more consumer-driven world, greed has been transformed into ambition, assertiveness, or even success. The yearning for more—more money, more prestige, more possessions—is seldom criticized unless it goes beyond grotesque proportions. However, greed is not just accumulation. Greed is accumulation without fulfillment. It is the hunger that increases with each feeding. A government worker who once accepted small favors can one day ask for huge kickbacks; a contractor who once jacked up numbers to get by can now overcharge to create empires. Greed is blind to reason, melts compassion, and turns people into relentless pursuers of profit—no matter what costs others.

And yet, fear is just as corrosive, although harder to find. Most do dirty things not to rise higher but to not sink lower. The worker who inflates performance reports is perhaps inflating them not to earn a bonus, but to keep from getting fired. The schoolteacher who takes bribes to pass a student may be afraid of retaliation from powerful parents or pressure from administrators to keep pass rates up. Fear masquerades as obedience. In highly hierarchical cultures, individuals are conditioned to comply rather than resist. They become tools of a system that insists on silent acquiescence. In such settings, integrity is smothered by fear. It teaches survival at the expense of self-respect.

Next comes insecurity—a much more insidious but no less potent motivator. Insecurity is not merely about material deprivation; it is the nagging uncertainty that one is never sufficient. It arises from a loss of faith—in oneself, in the justice of systems, in the future. Insecurity befalls both the powerful and the powerless. A bureaucrat who holds on to bribes fears becoming irrelevant upon retirement. A businessman who accumulates wealth in excess of use fears the volatility of markets or the uncertainty of governance. Even students, weighted down by societal pressures, might turn to cheating in examinations—not because they are lazy, but because they fear lagging behind. Insecurity narrows the moral horizon. It leads individuals to believe that ethics are a luxury only the secure can handle.

What is most striking is how these three forces—greed, fear, and insecurity—are usually created and maintained by societal institutions themselves. Economic inequality, for example, does not simply divide the rich and poor; it instills an emotional hierarchy of value. Those at the bottom internalize inadequacy. Those at the top fear being displaced. The end is a society in which everyone is seeking stability, but few are ever secure. Since as sociologist Zygmunt Bauman noted, "In a society of consumers, security becomes a product to be bought, not a condition to be cultivated."

This economy of emotions carries over into institutions. Political institutions reward opportunism; systems of education value scores over information; corporate frameworks reward profitability over morality. In these environments, greed is not met with punishment—it is encouraged. Fear is not soothed—it is manipulated. Insecurity is not remedied—it is exploited. And all these conditions condition corruption, institutionalizing it into everyday transactions until it is no longer perceived as anomalous and has become the norm.

But to limit corruption to individual shortcomings would be to overlook the bigger picture. The more profound question is not why individuals are greedy or afraid, but why systems are constructed so that these feelings become rational. Why should a parent feel compelled to offer a bribe to get their child into school? Why must a farmer bribe a clerk in order to get what is already rightfully theirs? Why must an exceptional researcher falsify data to achieve impossible publication quotas? They are not indications of personal moral deficiency—these are signals of a deteriorated social contract.

Education is capable of stepping into this emotional economy. Not only by the transfer of knowledge, but by the development of ethical literacy—an ability to question, reflect, and resist. Students need to be instructed not only in how systems function, but in how they should function. They need to be prepared not only with skills, but with moral courage. A curriculum that neglects the emotional basis of behavior cannot possibly develop character. But a classroom that becomes a place of dialogue, dignity, and discernment can make future citizens who are both competent and conscientious.

In order to deconstruct corruption, we need therefore to deal not just with actions, but with feelings. Greed has to be countered not with stigmatising desire but with cultivating satisfaction. Fear has to be dispelled not with empty promises but with instituting justice. Insecurity has to be cured not with empty slogans but with building actual opportunities and equitable systems.

In the end, corruption is not a policy failure—it is an imagination failure. It speaks to a world in which individuals cannot imagine a way to be successful without moral compromise. If we can design an education system that recaptures that imagination, then we can start substituting greed with generosity, fear with confidence, and insecurity with dignity.

## 2.3 Supply Meets Demand: Corruption as a Transaction

Corruption, by definition, is not an isolated act but a transaction—a negotiated agreement between two or more individuals in which legitimacy is traded for reciprocal, though frequently unequal, benefit. Easy as it is to place moral blame on the "corrupt actor," the fact is that corruption flourishes not alone but in conjunction. It is not an individual transgression; it is a market transaction. Like any transaction, it is dependent on supply and demand.

There has to be someone willing to offer the illegal favor, and another willing to pay for it. One group exercises control over access—be it to public goods, justice, schools, contracts, or power—and the other group wants that access, typically in an urgent way. This overlap generates a shadow economy alongside the official one, regulated not by fair rules but by rules of benefit. And as with any market, where there is demand, there will be supply.

This demand aspect of corruption tends to be the result of desperation or ambition. A parent wants a good school for their child but cannot leap over the bureaucratic obstacle without a bribe. A small business operator fed up with waiting months for a license makes an unofficial payment to hasten it. A politician is looking for good press and provides money or influence in exchange. These acts are not based solely on selfishness but on a belief—usually correct—that the official system is either slow or out of reach. When individuals believe that merit alone is not enough to advance them, when they sense the rules are broken or fixed, they start searching for "shortcuts"—what some economists refer to as "rational cheating."

On the demand side of this corrupt market are gatekeepers—individuals located inside the system who have discretionary control. They might be government ministers, corporate bosses, academic chancellors, or even policemen. They possess the control of benefits, permits, admissions, or licenses. For them, corruption is not only a personal opportunity but also an instrument of power. The power to grant favors or warp rules makes their status a commodity. And the more that the system is opaque, the greater the value of what they "sell."

This transactional model is ominously effective. It evolves, expands, and insinuates itself across tiers—from local bureaucracies to national institutions. What is even more perilous is that it assumes the veil of normalcy. In most locations, paying to have things done is no longer unusual—it's just how the game is played. A bribe is not corruption but a "service charge." Nepotism is not favoritism but "networking." Ghost workers on the payroll are not exceptions—they're plugged in along with every other overhead. The ethical boundaries are shifted by need and practice.

Economic theories sometimes talk of corruption as a market distortion, but perhaps more aptly, corruption is a market per se—one that forms when formal structures do not provide timely, equitable, or fair results. Where the visible hand of government falters, the invisible hand of corrupt trade becomes powerful.

Take the example of education. A rich parent donates to a school on the grounds of charity so that their child can get admitted. At face value, it is philanthropy. But in reality, it is an exchange. Limited seats are being sold under the guise of generosity. Apply the same reasoning to appointments, grading, scholarships, and grants for research. Every sphere becomes a market where merit is exchanged for influence, wealth, or affiliation. The marketization of possibility becomes both the commodity and the cost of corruption.

This transaction is further legitimized linguistically. The practice is cleaned up with euphemism: "influence fee," "influence," "understanding," or "setting." It is in such language that actors can intellectually disconnect from the wrongness of the act. It is an ethical choice, rather than an economic one. People start asserting, "Such is the nature of things around here," and "If not I, somebody else will." The transaction comes to be ritualized, with decreasing moral gravitas each time.

But this normalization is not without a price. Trust, the very foundation of any society, is silently eroded. When corruption becomes the default mode of behavior, it shreds the social contract. Individuals no longer trust that rules apply to everyone. Cynicism replaces faith in institutions. The young start believing that success is not determined by talent or effort but who you know and what you can afford. The outcome is not merely a loss of justice—it is a loss of hope.

At its core, corruption as a transaction is both cause and symptom. It is a symptom of systems that have not been responsive, inclusive, and just. And it is a cause of more dysfunction, generating more inequality, exclusion, and despair. This cycle is vicious—and enduring.

### So how do we stop it?

The response starts with understanding that corruption can't be fought by merely apprehending the criminals. We have to break the very incentives and institutions that ensure corruption as an available transaction. Mechanisms have to be made transparent.

Processes have to be streamlined. Public services have to be available. Whistleblowers need protection, not reprisals. And above all, education must impart not only competencies, but civic morals—enculcating the notion that equity is not a value, but a right.

Corruption as commerce flourishes in silence, in secrecy, in cynicism. It dies from the light of transparency, in dialogue, in moral clarity. By revealing to the world the nature of this market, and by recognizing the psychological and the systemic conditions necessary to support it, we first begin to move towards a rebirth of the world where justice is not an act of mercy to be purchased but a covenant to be enforced.

### 2.4 Scarcity, Power, and the Privilege to Break Rules

Scarcity is not just an economic condition but an ethical condition as well. When resources—tangible such as food, money, education, or intangible such as opportunities, justice, or dignity—are seen to be limited, human behavior changes fundamentally. During times of plenty, systems can be equitable. But during scarcity, rules tend to become secondary, and power starts to control access. It is under this crucible of scarce supply and uneven demand that corruption is created—not only as a single act of greed, but as a by-product of asymmetrical control. And with that control, the supreme privilege: to violate rules with impunity.

Limited supply, particularly in high-inequality societies, generates vicious competition not merely for survival but for progress. It compels people into ethical dilemmas in which ethics are balanced against necessity. But more insidiously, it gives disproportionate power to whoever has control over access to the scarce resource. Whether it's entry to prestigious schools, allocation of land, government contracts, health facilities, or appointments to jobs—those who hold power at the gateways start viewing rules as less boundaries and more bargains. Their capacity to selectively enforce, bend, or disregard rules becomes a new capital—one that is frequently more valuable than wealth itself.

In such an environment, power does not just equate to having resources. It equates to having the freedom to determine who receives what, when, and how. This freedom, when not held in check by accountability or transparency, becomes a fertile ground for corruption. It enables the privileged to transcend the rules, to function in a "state of exception," in the language of philosopher Giorgio Agamben, where ordinary laws are put on hold to serve the interests of the few. The irony is that the most powerful ones may need less to violate rules, yet enjoy most freedom to do so. And when they violate, it is not called corruption. It is wrapped rather in the guise of terms such as "executive decision," "strategic need," or "national interest."

The right to violate rules is not often distributed in a fair way. The poor are punished for minor violations—cutting a queue, having a false address to get their child into a better school, selling without a license. But the powerful and wealthy, who can embezzle millions or manipulate whole regulatory frameworks, tend to go scot-free or are even rewarded with promotion and accolades. This glaring disparity undermines not just public faith in institutions, but also discredits the very concept of justice. When citizens notice that the law is selectively enforced, that it is possible to avoid punishment through connections, and that the system bends at will for a fee or a favor, they no longer have faith in governance but even in morality.

Scarcity cuts this divide even more sharply. When public goods are in short supply—e.g., hospital beds in a pandemic, or employment slots in a shrinking economy—corruption is a natural response. Individuals start to think that the only means of getting what they require is through bribery, or bribery by influence, or lying. And individuals who can pay, or know who to speak to, start to think that rules are discretionary. They are not mistaken; the system inculcates this into them. The system rewards cunning rather than effort, closeness to power rather than skill.

Worst of all, it results in the normalization of rule-breaking. A school principal may take in more students than permitted, disregarding selection procedures, because a minister asked for it. A building company may overlook environmental standards because it has political influence. An exam paper may leak due to someone holding the keys finding profit more enticing than responsibility. In all these instances, the rule is not unclear—it is merely made irrelevant through the use of power.

What aggravates this crisis is the manner in which rule-breaking is legitimized in public life. Leaders in power justify their transgressions with stories of urgency, nationalism, religion, or development. They come across as exceptions—exempt from the law not because they defy it, but because they purport to act for a greater good. In this manner, rule-breaking is institutionalized, even celebrated. What starts as corruption turns into policy; what was initially secretive becomes tradition.

Education, unfortunately, is not exempt from this. Indeed, it is a fertile soil for such abuses. Powerful parents can get marks for their children by influence or intimidation. Research scholars can plagiarize due to pressure to publish, and administrators fudge data to get grants or accreditations. In all these instances, the lack of time, money, recognition, or future prospects compels individuals and institutions alike to sacrifice integrity. And those who obey the rules tend to be left behind, penalized not for evil but for their unwillingness to play the game.

But in the midst of all this, the most lethal corruption is not rule-breaking—but moral rule-bending. When the powerful repeatedly bend rules, society starts to re-tune its sense of what is acceptable. Young minds are especially susceptible to this change. They are growing up in a world where fairness appears to be quaint, where rule-bending is considered shrewd strategy, and where ethics are optional. This, in the long term, is a more destructive kind of corruption than any stolen fund—it is a corruption of conscience.

To counter this, we need not only to restore the rule of law but reassert the sanctity of rules themselves. Rules must not be instruments of oppression for the poor and playthings of convenience for the powerful. They must be a social contract based on equity, not exception. Transparency, accountability, and public participation are required—but not enough unless coupled with a moral awakening that reaffirms that no one is above the law, however noble the justification.

In a world that suffers from scarcity, going against rules can appear as the only means to an end. But unchallenged, this direction is not development, but ruin. For development founded on trampled rules is akin to a skyscraper constructed on a fissured foundation—quickly, it can reach great heights, but sooner or later, it will collapse. Genuine progress does not require shortcuts, but mechanisms that are just, equitable, and answerable to everyone.

**2.5 When Institutions Feed the Fire**

Institutions are typically hailed as the pillars of contemporary civilization—treasuries of order, stability, and reason. They are meant to act as impartial arbiters, ensuring that personal ambition is aligned with the greater good. But history and current reality time and again demonstrate that institutions, rather than dousing the fires of corruption, tend to fuel them. When bureaucracies are opaque, when justice systems move slowly or are partial, when schools and banks reward obedience above ability—corruption is not just a deviation; it takes on a life of its own within the institution itself.

The great economist Douglass North, a Nobel laureate for his contributions to the study of institutional economics, noted that institutions are "the rules of the game in a society." But what happens if the rules are designed to benefit a privileged minority? North cautions that when institutions are rigged to be in the interests of elites over the population, they stop mitigating uncertainty and start entrenching inequality. In these settings, corruption is not in spite of institutions—it thrives because of them.

Consider the judiciary, traditionally the last refuge of hope. When judgments take decades to come through, and verdicts are decided by political or economic influence, the notion of justice is undermined. Philosopher John Rawls, in his seminal A Theory of Justice, emphasized that justice is the first virtue of institutions.

A justice system that doesn't defend its most powerless cannot be deemed fair. And yet, when the legal process is bought and sold, and the price of bringing a lawsuit becomes prohibitively expensive, average citizens are not merely deprived of justice—they are specifically kept out of it.

Likewise, education, which ought to be a stairway to mobility, is regularly turned into a marketplace of privilege. Universities turn into degree-factories, curricula are defined by corporate sponsorship, and merit is subtly displaced by money and influence. As Amartya Sen points out in Development as Freedom, institutions ought to increase human capabilities. In reality, institutional gatekeeping tends to restrict access to quality education for marginalized groups, fostering cycles of exclusion and dependency. When admission, scholarship, or assessment is controlled through bribes or political intervention, educational institutions become party to the moral and economic corruption of society.

Political institutions are often too captive to special interests. The philosopher Antonio Gramsci outlined how ruling classes exert power not only through violence but through hegemony—by exercising influence on cultural and institutional norms in their favor. In contemporary democracies, this translates into the fact that elections, rather than being manifestations of popular will, tend to be reduced to spectacles paid for by secret donations and crony capitalism. Once in office, elected leaders can use state institutions to shore up patronage networks, entrenching themselves and punishing dissent.

Even regulatory agencies, established ostensibly to curb excesses, can become instruments of corruption. Since Nobel laureate George Stigler suggested in his Theory of Economic Regulation, regulators get "captured" by the respective industries that they are supposed to regulate. This "regulatory capture," as it is called, guarantees that policies and laws are made not for the benefit of people in general, but for the wealth of a few. When this happens in institutions that look after health, environment, education, or finance, results are disastrous and have consequences far-reaching in nature.

This institutional complicity is not necessarily overt. More often, it is hidden in thick layers of procedure, red tape, and deniability. Sociologist Max Weber, appreciative of bureaucratic efficiency, cautioned that rational-legal authority has a potential to become an "iron cage" of impersonal rules that stifle individuality and ethics. In such bureaucracies, corruption is not merely the exchange of bribes. It is not about making sure that systems are so complex, so impenetrable, that the only means of accomplishing anything is to "know someone" or "pay someone." So, corruption becomes institutionalized. It is the system, not an exception to it.

Public trust dissipates when institutions that vow justice, opportunity, and transparency consistently serve up favoritism, delay, and silence. The state's legitimacy, the sacredness of education, the moral fiber of the society—everything starts to crumble. Worse still, when the people witness institutions themselves being involved in or condoning corruption, they start to internalize it. There is a kind of moral numbness. As Hannah Arendt suggested in her investigation of totalitarianism, the evil of banality occurs when those who are imbedded within corrupt systems lose their capacity for moral thought and instead concern themselves with "just doing their job.

This kind of erosion is most perilous in developing cultures, where the institutions are only in the making and frequently missing are strong checks and balances. In such a setting, corruption is not only transactional—but transformational. It warps incentives, it discourages ethical participation, and it forces capability into exile or indifference. Accordingly, whole generations are socialized to distrust public institutions. Such distrust expresses itself in tax avoidance, low levels of civic involvement, voter abstinence, and a retreat from the democratic process itself.

The answer is not simple or quick. Reform has to be systemic. Transparency, digital governance, whistleblower protection, and citizen engagement are required—but they have to be supported by a profound moral renewal. Institutions need to be perceived again as not tools of domination but manifestations of collective will. They need to be responsive to the voices of the people they represent, particularly the most vulnerable.

As Frantz Fanon once put it, "Each generation must, out of relative obscurity, discover its mission, fulfill it, or betray it." Perhaps the mission of our generation is to take back institutions—not with words, but with resistance, reconstruction, and responsibility. Only so can we hope to put out the fires of corruption that these very same institutions, intentionally or unintentionally, have helped fan.

# III

# Systemic Design and Institutional Decay

Each institution starts with a vision—a dream built on social need, moral purpose, or economic expediency. Constitutions are written to lock in liberty and equality, schools are established to cultivate minds, judicial institutions are constructed to dispense justice, and bureaucracies are established to bring order from chaos. But eventually, the architecture that had supported a society can become its most inflexible limitation. What starts out as a virtuous plan can, in the absence of reform and watchfulness, devolve into a maze of inefficiency, injustice, and exclusion. This is the tragic irony of institutional change: the very institutions designed to benefit the public can become forces of its disempowerment.

Systemic decay is not an accident. It is frequently a creeping, invisible process, nested in routine processes in institutions, organizational culture, and bureaucratic momentum. It is different from observable corruption—such as bribery or theft—because it is structural. It is seen in policies that have lost their intent, in leaders more afraid of change than of failure, and in institutions more concerned with survival than with public service.

Among the first analyses of this phenomenon is that of Vilfredo Pareto, Italian economist and sociologist, who noted that elites in institutions are likely to function so as to maintain their own power and not the original objectives of the institution. These elite groups over time create what he termed "circulations of elites" in which one ruling group simply gives way to another without changing the underlying hierarchies and inequalities of the system. Institutions can appear different on the surface but their repressive structures persist.

This rot is most evident in systems of education. Schools and universities, ideally conceived as emancipatory spaces, all too frequently resemble bureaucratic silos. Curriculum stagnation, politicization of pedagogy, commercialization of degrees, and over-reliance on rote testing create an environment in which certification becomes more important than learning. The concept of education as a tool of enlightenment is gradually being replaced by its role as a credentialing machine. As Ivan Illich claimed in Deschooling Society, schools usually reinforce a non-obvious curriculum of consumerism, competition, and conformity over critical thinking and human growth.

This problem is not just about education, however. Health systems, intended to promote dignity and care, too often serve profit or bureaucracy instead. Judicial systems, intended to promote fairness, become unreachable through procedural barriers or the costs of accessing them. Welfare programs, designed to combat poverty, are captured by middlemen. This is not just a breakdown of personal morality, but a breakdown of institutional logic. Systems rot when they become out of sync between their structure, their purpose, and their moral compass.

The noted economist Mancur Olson, in his book The Rise and Decline of Nations, had contended that as institutions grow older, they develop "distributional coalitions"—interest groups that oppose change to preserve their privileges. These groups, while small in numbers, have disproportionate influence and discourage innovation and reform. Institutional sclerosis is the consequence, where change becomes not only hard but risky to entrenched interests.

This is why reforms to make something more transparent, decentralized, or citizen-centric are usually thwarted by incumbents. These incumbents have no reason to repair a system that benefits them, even if it doesn't benefit society. Therefore, the longer an institution endures without reform, the more likely it will turn toward serving itself instead of its intended purpose.

Institutional decline also occurs at the level of psychology and culture. Institutional decline generates cynicism, disillusionment, and disillusionment in the public space. When public institutions delay, humiliate, or discriminate against citizens, the latter internalize helplessness. They start regarding failure of systems as inevitable and corruption as standard. This demoralization nurtures a process in which civic disengagement in turn decays institutions further, generating a feedback loop of malady.

Philosopher Jürgen Habermas explained this as the "legitimation crisis" of modern institutions: when institutions' promise and performance gap is too large, public trust erodes. If institutions lack legitimacy, they lose their moral mandate, and decisions—even if they are legally enforceable—fail to command respect. In these conditions, citizens resort to substitute sources of authority—identity, religion, populism, or patronage—that erode democratic governance itself.

Another reason that institutions rot is because they're usually constructed with reference to a world that ceased to be some time ago. Bureaucratic styles fashioned during the industrial era refuse to fit within the digital order. Regulatory constructs tailored to fit national economies fail to address such transnational imperatives as global warming, online privacy, or capital flows between nations. This has been called by the philosopher Zygmunt Bauman the condition of "liquid modernity," where institutions are firm, but the world surrounding them becomes more fluid and volatile.

And yet, reform is possible. But it has to start by imagining institutions as dynamic systems, not static structures. That requires going beyond cosmetic changes—new slogans, reshuffles, or policy tweaks—and embracing systemic reengineering. Institutions need to be made transparent, participatory, and accountable. They need to shift their goals from control to service, from compliance to compassion, from hierarchy to horizontal engagement.

This change must be achieved with civic imagination and moral courage. As Elinor Ostrom, the sole woman to have been awarded the Nobel Prize in Economics, showed through her research on common-pool resources, people can build decentralized, self-managed institutions that are efficient as well as just. The solution is to engage stakeholders in the formulation and enforcement of rules. This realization does not apply merely to forests or fisheries but also to education, health, and public finance.

In the end, institutions mirror the societies that construct and support them. If they are to be just, inclusive, and resilient, then citizens need to be engaged actors, not passive recipients. Civic literacy, democratic dialogue, and moral clarity are as crucial to institutional reform as policy innovation or technological upgrade.

To let institutions decay is to default on the social compact. To mend them is to recapture our collective will. And in that fight is not only the redemption of systems, but the renewal of society itself.

**3.1 How Systems Create Loopholes by Design**

Systems are viewed as impartial buildings regulated by law, rules, and processes. But beyond the seeming impartiality of institutions, there exists a much more devious and complex reality. Systems are not always constructed to cut out corruption—sometimes, they institutionalize it. Loopholes, rather than mistakes, are actually purposeful provisions built into systems by people of power, influence, and vision. These are the hidden back roads on which corruption flows free.

In an Indian context, the term "Hindu rate of growth" was first used by late economist Prof. Raj Krishna, who also noted that most of India's economic stagnation in the post-independence period was the result of bureaucratic inertia and what he termed "permit-license raj." This mesh of permissions, licenses, and quotas was initiated in the garb of socialism and regulation, but it necessarily created discretionary powers and access networks that were informal. Rules got selectively enforced, and political and economic capitals could bend the system. The loopholes, in that way, were systemic rather than aberrations that happened to be part of the design.

Indian philosopher and political theorist Dr. Bhikhu Parekh has pointed out how power relations in post-colonial nations tend to internalise colonial hierarchies, giving rise to institutions that entrench inequality and do not eliminate it. In his musings on multiculturalism and government, Parekh observes that rules can seem democratic but actually work in very exclusionary ways. The design of these rules, the wording of policy, and the degree of interpretive latitude—all provide channels for privileged actors to circumvent norms under legal cover.

Let us look at the Indian tax system. Although looking equal and just, its complexity over time has enabled high-net-worth individuals and companies to dodge their rightful portion of taxes. The Kaldor Committee Report (1956), spearheaded by British economist Nicholas Kaldor at the Indian government's request, underscored the manner in which tax legislation must be simplified in order to deter evasion. Yet one reform after another seldom touched upon structural loopholes—such as agricultural income exemptions being exploited by urban elites or excessively liberal depreciation allowances to firms. Indian economist Dr. Arun Kumar, in his writings on the black economy, has consistently demonstrated how these systemic designs are responsible for almost 50% of India's GDP being unaccounted for—driven by loopholes built into financial and administrative systems.

Loopholes also result from administrative discretion. As Dr. Pranab Bardhan, a well-known development economist, points out, India's bureaucracy is both over-regulating and under-capable. Policies are framed with broad discretion vested in the officials, particularly at the state and district levels. This scope for discretion together with inadequate systems of accountability leaves room for arbitrariness at the benefit of those who "know how" to "manage" the system. The end product is not just corruption but the institutionalisation of corrupt procedures as survival strategies or ways of working.

Again, Indian sociologist Prof. André Béteille delivers a key to the sociology of institutions. He contends that most Indian institutions have a twin nature—one being formal and the other being informal. Although formal organizations focus on merit, procedure, and legality, the informal setup usually relies on patronage, caste alliances, and one's personal contacts. The interoperation between these two levels offers fertile ground for corrupt tendencies with loopholes being the meeting point where legality is warped by social capital. In his book, Béteille alerts that institutional degradation sets in as informal logic trumps formal rules, a quietly facilitated process through systemic design.

A salient instance can be found in public procurement and infrastructure construction. Tenders are advertised with impenetrable eligibility criteria, amorphous definition of scope, and watered-down penalty clauses. They permit the picking and choosing of favored bidders or project deferments without proportional sanctions. Frequently justified on grounds of flexibility or convenience, such vagueness invites inflationary bills, shoddy work, and collusion between government servants and private contractors. No wonder the reports of the Comptroller and Auditor General (CAG) are frequently filled with instances of cost overruns and procedural irregularities that rarely get prosecuted. These are not failures—these are products of systems intended to serve a select few in the guise of legality.

Even in education—a field touted for being enlightened—policy loopholes abound. The Right to Education Act (RTE) ensures 25% reservation for economically weaker sections in private schools, yet many schools sidestep this by adjusting admission standards or stating non-availability of infrastructure. Regulatory uncertainty and absence of enforcement structures enable elite institutions to violate law in practice while looking compliant in form. As Prof.

Krishna Kumar, former NCERT director, remarks, education inequality in India is sustained not merely by access or affordability but by institutional frameworks that enable the elite to design parallel schooling arrangements—commonly in the guise of excellence.

The deeper issue arises when such loopholes become normalized. The experience of navigating, exploiting, or profiting from such systemic loopholes is embedded in the institutional culture over time. This is how corruption becomes entrenched, not as a momentary lapse but as an unspoken tradition transmitted across generations of administrators, professionals, and citizens. Social psychologist and public intellectual Prof. Ashis Nandy describes this moral indecision by the concept of "intimate enemies," whereby the colonized absorb the skein of corrupt rationality of the colonizer. A system thus develops where rule-breaking becomes a display of cleverness, and honesty is perceived as naivety.

The urgent task, then, is not so much to plug loopholes, but to lay bare the motives behind them. Systemic reform has to move beyond mere surface-level restructuring; it has to question the values, interests, and assumptions on which systems are constructed. As Dr. B.R. Ambedkar warned in his constituent assembly speech, "however good a Constitution may be, it is sure to turn out bad because those who are called to work it happen to be a bad lot." Systemic reform, therefore, is not merely about amending laws—it's about altering the moral ecology in which laws are enacted and enforced.

Loopholes do not come into existence by chance. They are born of compromise between power and principle, between the rule of law and the rule of convenience. The ultimate test of the ethical basis of a society is not how many rules it possesses, but how honestly those rules are created and applied. As long as systems are designed to benefit some and to mislead others, education alone will not be enough to empower. It has to be accompanied by moral courage and common vigilance in order to construct institutions anew from scratch.

### 3.2 Bureaucracy, Red Tape, and Rent-Seeking

Bureaucracy, which has been considered the cornerstone of contemporary governance, has the purpose of maintaining transparency, equity, and efficiency in managing policies and laws. Yet in much of the world, and particularly in post-colonial societies like India, those very institutions which are supposed to be working for the public end up becoming tools for the sustenance of inefficiency, corruption, and exploitation. Bureaucracy, by virtue of its structural inflexibility and procedural intricacy, has provided fertile ground for red tape and rent-seeking activities.

In the case of a developing nation such as India, the growth of bureaucracy has a colonial heritage. When the British ruled India, the Indian Civil Services were structured to advance the colonial regime, focusing on control and surveillance. However, the continued presence of this system in post-independence India has been a two-edged sword. Though bureaucracy in theory provides continuity, stability, and impartial application of government policy, it tends to become a self-serving, opaque, and slow-moving system. What ensues is a complex mesh of rules and regulations that inhibit progress as well as enable rent-seeking behavior.

### *The Bureaucratic Machine: Function and Dysfunction*

The primary function of any bureaucracy is to execute public policy in an efficient and equitable manner. Ideally, it is an impartial arbiter between the citizen and the state, so that decisions are reached in accordance with rules and law. In actuality, though, bureaucratic establishments in India, as Dr. Rajni Kothari establishes in his definitive writings on Indian democracy, find themselves mired in a complicated web of inefficiency and bias. Kothari observes that the pervasive centralization of authority in bureaucratic systems in India has resulted in a "mono-bureaucratic" state, in which decision-making is concentrated in a narrow, insulated group of elites. This centralization suppresses initiative at lower levels of government, resulting in delays, and inefficiency, and providing the opportunity for corruption.

The phrase "red tape" is often used to characterize excessive bureaucracy and unnecessary regulations that slow down decision-making. In India, red tape tends to result from the absence of coordination between departments, too much documentation needed, and the lack of transparency in procedures. Prof. Amartya Sen, a prominent economist and philosopher, in his seminal book Development as Freedom, refers to the suffocating impact that inefficiencies in the bureaucracy can have on the economic and social growth of a nation. Sen stresses that over-bureaucracy and administrative hurdles erode the ability of people to act, as they have to make their way through a maze of approvals and permits that eventually stall productivity and economic development.

### Red Tape and Corruption: A Symbiotic Relationship

Red tape does not only generate inefficiencies—it also fosters corruption. Bureaucratic processes, when too complex, tend to require unofficial "favors" or bribes in lieu of skipping delays and obstacles. This leads to a self-reinforcing circle in which people, firms, or organizations are forced to rent-seek to gain benefits or avoid penalties for violating complicated rules. Dr. M. N. Srinivas, an Indian sociologist, contended that the expansion of bureaucracy in post-independence India produced a new group of "power brokers"—people who gained from their capacity to navigate through or go around the bureaucratic labyrinth.

The bureaucratic labyrinth usually takes the shape of licenses, permits, and regulations that provide bureaucrats with discretion in their application. This discretion, if not checked, results in what sociologists such as Prof. André Béteille refer to as "bureaucratic patronage." Bureaucrats employ their office not to serve the public but to preserve their status by selectively enforcing the rules to favor some individuals or groups. The general public usually has no option but to turn to bribery or "gifting" favors to hasten services, hence promoting rent-seeking behavior.

The concept of rent-seeking, initially described by economist Gordon Tullock in the 1960s and further developed by Anne Krueger, is the phenomenon whereby people or institutions try to acquire riches without adding any value. This usually occurs by manipulation of the political or economic system with a view to obtaining advantages like government contracts, monopolistic benefits, or exemption from regulations. For India, rent-seeking has been institutionalized in the form of the permit-license raj, with the latter permitting the well-connected to acquire favors, subsidies, or benefits, with often public welfare as the casualty.

### *Rent-Seeking in India: The Permits, Licenses, and Quotas System*

Traditionally, the economic system of India was dominated by a myriad of regulations governing almost every facet of economic existence. The Industrial Policy Resolution of 1956, effective for more than a few decades, placed industrial sectors under the control of the government, compelling firms to acquire licenses and permits prior to starting operations. These regulations provided fertile ground for rent-seeking, as companies and individuals competed not on innovation or efficiency, but on their capacity to obtain these approvals and licenses. This system, far from stimulating real economic development, was in large measure designed to enrich those who could successfully navigate the maze of bureaucracy.

At this period, the "license raj" became one with corruption. Politicians and bureaucrats regulated access to resources, and companies were required to pay bribes or provide political favors in order to acquire the required licenses. This led to an artificial shortage in the economy, where expansion was limited by bureaucratic hurdles. Dr. Bibek Debroy, who is an Indian economist and public policy analyst, in his essays on the economic costs of bureaucratic delays, points out that the license raj directly led to India's retarded economic growth in the first few decades of independence.

The liberalization of the Indian economy in the early 1990s saw the removal of most of these barriers. Rent-seeking behavior, however, did not cease; instead, it mutated into new forms. Opening of industries like real estate, infrastructure, and telecommunication opened doors for rent-seeking as private businesses tried to maneuver the regulatory conditions to win pleasing policies or a contract. Special mention has to be made regarding the expansion of public-private partnership (PPP) schemes due to its effects in establishing novel avenues of rent-seeking as there is room to extract rents as politicians and bureaucrats have their finger in the pie while crafting deals.

### The Moral and Economic Implications of Rent-Seeking

Rent-seeking is very seriously immoral and economically injurious. Economically, it results in allocative inefficiency—resources get wasted not on their most valuable use but on the basis of who is able to obtain them through political or bureaucratic means. According to Dr. Jagdish Bhagwati, one of India's leading economists, rent-seeking diverts resources from productive investments and innovation and therefore slows overall economic growth, as he has put forth in his writings on trade and development.

Moral repercussions are just as extreme. Rent-seeking degrades the legitimacy of government, as the people begin to perceive the government not as an impartial mediator but as a scheme to reward the strong and penalize the weak. This diminishes faith in the institutions of democracy, contributing to cynicism and disillusion. Dr. B. R. Ambedkar, in his contribution to social justice and equality, pinned his argument that corruption within institutions enhances social inequality and hinders the prospects of society's development. If rulers are permitted to distort the rules to favor themselves, it sustains the status quo of inequality and marginalization and denies the most vulnerable members of society access to important resources and opportunities.

In addition, as Indian historian and sociologist Prof. Ramachandra Guha has written in his works on Indian political and social history, rent-seeking perpetuates systemic injustice. By channeling resources and power into the hands of a limited number of people, rent-seeking culture erodes democratic accountability, resulting in cycles of exploitation and stagnation.

### Breaking the Cycle of Bureaucratic Rent-Seeking

Breaking the cycle of red tape and bureaucracy and rent-seeking involves a complete overhaul of the system, not merely the laws and regulations, but the structure and operation of institutions as well. According to Dr. Amartya Sen, development cannot be limited to economic growth; it has to be concerned with the widening of individual freedoms and opportunities. This entails an atmosphere where corruption is neither institutionalized nor normalized. Dr. Pratap Bhanu Mehta, one of India's leading political theorists, recommends institutionalizing accountability, decentralizing power, and simplifying regulations as essential to breaking the nexus of red tape and rent-seeking.

Ultimately, it is apparent that the bureaucracy, when left to run amok, generates inefficiency and corruption. Red tape, instead of being a necessary tool for governance, becomes an instrument for rent-seeking activities. In order to build a more transparent and equitable society, it is necessary to make sure that the bureaucratic machinery operates in a way that promotes the public interest, not private interests.

### 3.3 Collusion and Crony Capitalism

Crony capitalism is a word that has become more and more prominent in the debate on economic inequality, political influence, and corruption. It describes an economic system in which business success is determined by close ties between government officials and business leaders. This is a far cry from the ideal of a free market, where competition, innovation, and efficiency are the driving forces. In crony capitalism, companies succeed not due to market competition or the quality of their products and services, but due to their capacity to use political connections and gain favor with the ruling elite.

Crony capitalism has prospered in most emerging economies, including India, to create a culture in which businesses and the political elite collaborate on mutual advantages at the cost of the wider population. The complex web of politics and business tycoons results in economic growth that is meritless, but rather depends on the power of the elite to control state assets, bend regulations, and obtain monopolistic licenses or contracts.

The origins of crony capitalism are usually traceable to poor institutional structures and governance systems. When the regulatory systems of the state are unclear or selectively applied, the entry is opened for those with the appropriate connections to take advantage of these loopholes for their own benefit. Perhaps the most pernicious thing about crony capitalism is the way it destroys the ideals of fairness and competition in the market. Rather than competition on the basis of innovation, quality, and consumer choice, the market turns into a war zone for political favors. In such a system, firms are not necessarily the most efficient or the best but the most politically well-connected, and this results in stagnation in innovation and uneven allocation of resources.

In India, crony capitalism has a long tradition, and its origins date back to the initial years of post-independence economic policy. During the post-independence period, the government pursued a model of state-led development with extensive regulation of industries like industry, infrastructure, and trade. Although the policy was intended to safeguard infant industries and achieve balanced growth, the regime permitted plenty of scope for crony capitalism and rent-seeking. The well-known "License Raj," which was in place between the 1950s and the 1990s, entrenched a regime under which companies needed government licenses to conduct business, grow, or bring in foreign products. This provided bureaucrats and politicians with immense latitude in determining who would be able to do business and who would not. Consequently, a majority of companies thrived not due to their competitive strengths but due to their success in getting preferential treatment from the state.

The mutually beneficial relationship between business elites and government elites created a collusion-corruption cycle. Political figures and bureaucrats were able to provide businesses with access to limited resources, exclusive deals, or advantageous regulations in return for bribes, political contributions, or other types of kickbacks. This mechanism developed so-called rent-seeking behavior, under which companies go about trying to get economic returns through political system manipulation instead of competition in the marketplace. Eventually, such systems ensure inequality since wealth and power tend to fall into the hands of a small group of influential individuals and corporations.

The impact of crony capitalism is very significant. On an economic basis, it generates inefficiency and misallocation of resources. When companies are selected on political grounds instead of merit, it hinders more competent or creative companies from prospering. Customers lose out in the form of higher prices and poor-quality goods and services since companies that end up succeeding in the market may not be the most competitive but politically connected ones. This acts as a barrier to entry for smaller companies or new companies which could otherwise introduce innovation and new ideas into the market.

Politically, crony capitalism undermines democratic accountability. As politicians and business elites become close, the public's interests get marginalized. Politicians can prioritize their business associates' needs ahead of the well-being of the public, making decisions that will advance the interest of a narrow, privileged elite while disregarding the public good. Further, if businesses are sustained by political patronage instead of market performance, the political process is more vulnerable to corruption. Crony capitalism fosters a culture of impunity, with government leaders and business tycoons acting with impunity because their shared interests insulate them from accountability.

Socially, the impact of crony capitalism is also dire. As economic and political power concentrate in the hands of a few, the social compact between the state and society erodes. Inequality increases, and social mobility becomes harder. The very essence of democratic rule – to provide equal opportunities to everyone – is defeated by a system that benefits the elite at the expense of the masses. This leads to instability in society, as people become frustrated with the absence of opportunities and the continuation of corruption.

Collusion is a critical element of crony capitalism, the practice whereby companies or company executives, in league with government officials, indulge in illegal or unethical behavior to advance their own interests. Collusion can manifest itself in various ways, such as price-fixing, bid-rigging, and market manipulation or regulation. In most instances, corruption among business executives and government officials guarantees that specific businesses or individuals gain access to high-paying government contracts, evade regulation, or dominate markets, much to the disadvantage of consumers and other companies.

Collusion under crony capitalism forms a vicious cycle where the state and private sector are mutually dependent on each other's success. This dependence makes the system of rent-seeking and corruption more robust because it becomes more challenging for both parties to confront the status quo without compromising their own interests. For example, if a government official were to reveal corruption or cronyism, they may lose patronage from the business elite who may, in return, employ their influence to destroy the official's political career. Similarly, entrepreneurs who profit from crony transactions might not want to criticize government corruption for fear that their profits and market position would be threatened.

The concept of a "free market" is undermined by the crony capitalist system. Ideally, a free market would be regulated by the principles of supply and demand, where companies compete on the basis of innovation and customer satisfaction. But in a crony capitalist economy, market results are determined more by political favors and backroom bargains than by the forces of competition and merit. As economist Joseph Stiglitz has noted in his criticism of market economies, crony capitalism warps the market, resulting in inefficient economic results and preventing the free market from working as it should. In his book, Globalization and Its Discontents, Stiglitz points to the ways in which the neglect of cronyism in markets results in greater inequality, erodes the quality of governance, and harms the legitimacy of democratic institutions.

Not only does crony capitalism hinder economic growth, but it also erodes the social fabric of a nation. When individuals realize that success in business is achieved by means of political relationships instead of work and ingenuity, it undermines faith in government and weakens social cohesion. This is especially harmful for developing nations, where economic disparities and social stratification are already pressing issues. Dr. Amartya Sen states that inequality should be decreased for economic development as well as for democracy. Without an even playing field, where companies come and go depending on their worth, not political ties, the economic and social gap between the poor and rich widens, causing dissatisfaction and unrest.

The existence of crony capitalism in India has been made worse by a number of structural issues. The nation's political scene, with frequent coalition governments, can breed the kind of scenario where political parties become heavily dependent on financial support from rich business interests. That, in its turn, contributes to a quid pro quo relationship in which politicians gain special policies for the business leaders in return for vote support. The political economy in such a system gets entangled with private interests, and it becomes hard to distinguish between politics and business.

Although India's economic liberalization during the 1990s brought substantial growth, it also opened up new avenues for cronyism. Privatization of state-owned enterprises, deregulation of some sectors, and opening up the economy to international markets created new opportunities for rent-seeking. The fast development of sectors like real estate, telecommunications, and infrastructure has given sufficient scope for businesses to approach politicians and bureaucrats to seek favors, further consolidating the nexus between business and political elites.

The eradication of crony capitalism needs systemic and institutional change. The state needs to take positive measures to curb corruption, enhance transparency, and impose accountability in public as well as private sectors. Strengthening institutions of regulation, guaranteeing the independence of the judiciary, and upholding the rule of law are crucial in checking business elites' attempts to dominate and bend the system to their advantage. In addition, public consciousness and active participation of citizens are needed to address the culture of cronyism that has penetrated so deeply across much of the globe.

Finally, crony capitalism is a complete failure of the free market system and a corruption of democratic principles. It enables a tiny elite to acquire disproportionate power and wealth at the expense of the majority. In order to really move ahead, societies need to tackle the underlying causes of cronyism, so that economic and political systems work to benefit the many, not the few. That is when a free and competitive marketplace can be achieved, as well as with it, a more equitable and just society.

### 3.4 Welfare and Public Scheme Corruption

One of the most pernicious sorts of corruption is welfare and public scheme corruption, which targets the weakest sections of society—the poor, the aged, women, children, marginalized groups, and those that are dependent on state aid for survival. Welfare programs are, by their nature, supposed to be redistributive mechanisms for correcting structural disadvantage and offering protection to citizens in the form of a safety net. But the moment corruption becomes a part of this space, the very goal of these schemes is destroyed. It not just results in monetary loss to the state but leads to severe social and moral cost by destroying people's faith and perpetuating structural exclusion.

In the Indian scenario, welfare corruption assumes diverse forms—ghost beneficiaries, misappropriation of funds, over-invoicing of inputs, bribe-giving for entitlements, and leakage of food grains or other material benefits even before they are delivered to the target groups. Welfare programs such as the Public Distribution System (PDS), Mahatma Gandhi National Rural Employment Guarantee Act (MGNREGA), and the Mid-Day Meal Scheme have been vision-ary in intent but fragile in implementation. A huge web of middlemen and discretionary control over means has provided avenues for leakage, siphoning, and favoritism.

The Planning Commission had sometime in the past put an estimate at which less than 15 paise out of a rupee spent by the government on the poor actually went to the poor. This much-quoted figure (popularized by Rajiv Gandhi) came to represent the inefficiency and corruption built into public distribution systems. Even with intensive efforts over recent years to make things more transparent—e.g., direct benefit transfers (DBTs), payments through Aadhaar, and recording of accounts—a new kind of corruption continues unabated. Beneficiaries now increasingly pay backhand commissions, rather than in the open thievery from the past. Local patronages, political allegiance, and governmental gatekeeping muddy the waters additionally.

A key contributing factor is the imbalance of information and power between the state and the people. Most poor and marginalized individuals are ignorant of their rights or too afraid of authority to question it. Bureaucratic discretion without accountability becomes a ground for extortion. The issue is not necessarily the lack of resources but in last-mile delivery, as Indian sociologist Jean Drèze has frequently illustrated in his work on rural poverty and welfare systems. Drèze, and economist Amartya Sen, highlighted in An Uncertain Glory: India and Its Contradictions that India's development success is undermined by bad governance and weak public services, especially in education, health, and social security.

The targeting problem is also plagued by corruption. Beneficiary lists are often manipulated according to political allegiances, caste equations, or bribes. The ones who are to be excluded end up being included by document forgery or by bribes, while the actual beneficiaries are denied. This not only leads to wastage of public money but also increases resentment and suspicion in communities. Welfare gets politicized, and the ruling parties make use of schemes as instruments of patronage and not as means of justice.

In India, for example, research on MGNREGA has shown how job cards are being provided to phony individuals, wages are being diverted by contractors and local functionaries, and attendance registers are being forged. In most instances, workers claim to have worked fewer days than they are documented for, with part of their wages going to middlemen. Likewise, the National Rural Health Mission has witnessed procurement scams, over-billing for medical devices, and delivery of spurious medicines in various states.

The leakage and corruption in the PDS is a case in itself. Decades of reform have failed to end large-scale diversion of subsidized food grains into the system. Poor people's grains are being sold in the open market or stocked by corrupt dealers, while bureaucrats and politicians are party to many such transactions. While digital ration cards and GPS tracking of trucks have added some degree of transparency, the implementation remains patchy across states.

Theoretically, institutional economics helps explain why welfare programs are particularly prone to corruption. Institutions structure human behavior, and under weak institutional conditions—low accountability, bad monitoring, and excessive discretion—the reward to cheat exceeds the cost of being caught. Nobel Prize winner Douglass North maintained that whenever informal norms and formal rules converge, corruption gets institutionalized. In the context of welfare programs, the official rules (like eligibility conditions or procedural protections) are frequently evaded by a network of unofficial practices—bribes, nepotism, coercion—that go unchecked because of social hierarchies and absence of redressal mechanisms.

The behavioral aspects of welfare corruption are also significant. Once corruption is institutionalized—as something "everyone does"—it ceases to carry a stigma and becomes a way of life. Street-level bureaucrats who are responsible for the delivery of welfare might rationalize bribe-taking as payment for low salaries or as a function of the "system." Citizens, in return, internalize the notion that one has to "pay to get anything done," thus creating a cycle of dependency and moral compromise. This erosion of morals is especially risky because it involves society's most vulnerable ethical space—care for the poor and vulnerable.

Indian philosopher Ramachandra Gandhi once cautioned that the decay of compassion and public conscience is a more perilous kind of social decay than sheer inefficiency. When welfare programs get corrupted, the notion of a moral state—that cares for, protects, and nurtures—slowly dies. Welfare corruption, in this sense, is not only a failure of governance; it is a spiritual crisis of the modern nation-state.

International comparisons shed additional light. Such countries as Brazil and Mexico, where conditional cash transfers including Bolsa Família and Oportunidades have been introduced, have proven that with appropriate combinations of openness, grass-roots participation, and information technologies, welfare can be transferred efficiently with minimal corruption. They are continually audited, engage grass-roots communities in monitoring, and utilize biometric and banking technology to pay the benefits directly into the hands of women household heads. Conversely, the Indian welfare architecture, while improving, continues to face fragmented governance and vested interests at the local level.

One means of fighting welfare corruption is by enhancing social audits and citizen engagement. Efforts such as Mazdoor Kisan Shakti Sangathan (MKSS) in Rajasthan have led the way in community auditing of public works and entitlements, compelling officials to be accountable through public hearings. Such efforts demonstrate that once individuals are enabled to watch over the system, corruption is increasingly difficult to keep under wraps. Legislation like the Right to Information (RTI) has also been instrumental in exposing malfeasance in welfare schemes, although moves to weaken such legislation are ominous signs of a retreat from openness.

In addition, technology can serve a dual purpose. While Aadhaar-based biometric authentication and digitization have facilitated delivery, they also create new modes of exclusion and data abuse. For instance, several elderly or disabled beneficiaries in far-flung locations experience biometric matching difficulty, resulting in ration or pension denial. This once again demonstrates that technical solutions cannot substitute for ethical governance and human-centric design.

Ultimately, the integrity of welfare and public schemes rests on the moral will of the state and the collective conscience of society. If the poor must pay a price for every morsel of food, every job guarantee, or every educational aid, then the very foundation of the welfare state is compromised. As Mahatma Gandhi succinctly put it, "A nation's greatness is measured by how it treats its weakest members." In not permitting corruption to brew in the welfare programs, we don't just deprive the poor of their entitlement, but also dispossess ourselves of our own moral right to be.

In conclusion, corruption in the welfare schemes isn't merely about money loss—It's a violation of the concept of justice, equality, and democracy. Fixing it involves not only improved systems and tighter legislation but a cultural and moral shift in how we think about state-citizen relations. Welfare is not charity or favor but a right, and any breach of that right has to be considered a serious injustice, not an administrative oversight.

### 3.5 The Cost of Corruption: Who Pays and How

Corruption, in its nature, distorts resource allocation, undermines public trust, and undermines institutions. But to fully comprehend its seriousness, the question must be asked: who pays the price of corruption, and how? The response, though appearing obvious, becomes a multifaceted and nuanced reality where the poorest members of society pay the greatest price, and where the harm caused is not only economic but also moral, institutional, and intergenerational.

At the most visible level, corruption imposes a direct financial burden on the common citizen. When public officials demand bribes for routine services—be it a ration card, a driving license, or a hospital bed—the citizen is forced to pay twice: once through taxes and again through illicit payments. These costs are especially severe for the poor, who tend to live on tenuous incomes and have little ability to absorb such shocks. In a Transparency International survey, more than 50% of Indians who had used a government service in the past year said they paid a bribe. This results in a regressive system in which the price of public services is disproportionately higher for the economically weaker sections.

But the indirect costs are much more calamitous. Corruption increases the cost of public capital—roads, schools, bridges, water supply—through kickbacks, inferior materials, and padded contracts. It doesn't simply translate to wasted money; it leads to inadequate public goods, collapsing buildings, washed-away roads, and failing water supplies. Indian economist Bibek Debroy has maintained that corruption decreases the efficiency of capital spending, producing what is referred to as a "leakage multiplier," whereby the actual value of each rupee spent diminishes significantly because of theft and inefficiency.

Further, corruption deters investment, both domestic and foreign, by creating uncertainty and risk. Nobody wants to traverse a bribe jungle, a maze of vague rules, and discretionary rule-making. Nobel Prize-winning economist Joseph Stiglitz stressed that corruption is in effect a "tax on investment," warping incentives and promoting rent-seeking rather than innovation and productivity. In corrupt societies, even the best-designed policies are doomed because their implementation is tainted. It is as if designing an ideal machine but allowing it to operate on dirty oil.

Perhaps the most pernicious effects of corruption are on human development indicators. Money intended for schools never reaches the classrooms; mid-day meals are diverted by corrupt contractors; vital medicines never find their way to rural health centers. Thus, generations of children grow up undernourished and undereducated, perpetuating a vicious cycle of poverty. Indian development economist Jean Drèze has documented, through many field studies, how corruption in social services such as education and health care imposes a silent, invisible tax on the poor that is paid in terms of their future.

Corruption also imposes a gigantic psychological cost. It generates cynicism, apathy, and a culture of helplessness. When individuals think that merit is inconsequential, that rules are intended to be disobeyed, and that influence trumps integrity, they lose confidence in the social contract. Citizens disengage, elections are de-legitimized, and democratic institutions become empty shells. The renowned Indian sociologist G.S. Ghurye cautioned that when institutions are disconnected from ethical and moral foundations, social cohesion starts breaking down. Corruption is not merely a deviation from rules; it is a collapse of the moral order that binds citizens to the state and to one another.

The cost to the environment is also massive. When environmental clearances are awarded in return for bribes, forests are cut down, rivers are poisoned, and ecosystems are destroyed irretrievably. The long-term bill for this damage is paid by not the corporations or officials that facilitate it, but by common people—particularly indigenous peoples, small farmers, and coming generations. Corruption in this way is also an intergenerational plunder, robbing not only of the current but of the unborn.

Corruption also weakens state capacity. If public institutions fall under the control of vested interests, they lose the capacity to provide justice, uphold the law, or implement the rules. The police turn partisan, the judiciary clogged and distorted, and the bureaucracy demoralized. The price here is the very legitimacy of the state. As Dr. B.R. Ambedkar cautioned, the fibre of democracy will not be able to endure if social and economic justice is not delivered. Corruption guarantees precisely that: denial of justice both in visible and invisible forms.

Additionally, corruption worsens inequality. Corruption provides the rich and powerful with means to twist rules to their advantage—land grabbing, cornering contracts, tax evasion—while the poor are punished for mere violations. As the economist Thomas Piketty has demonstrated in his worldwide research on inequality, untrammeled capital accumulation without institutional restraints creates structural inequality and undermines democratic foundations. In a corrupt regime, privilege accumulates while vulnerability increases. In this way, corruption is not only a crime—it is a violence against equity and justice.

The last cost is possibly the most tragic: the normalization of wrongdoing. If we raise our children in a society where corruption is the norm, where success is envied regardless of methods, and where integrity is equated with naiveté, then we undermine the very principles that hold civilization together. Corruption is not merely an economic or political issue—it is a challenge to civilization. Corruption undermines the moral sense of society and recasts the concept of success in forms that strip us of our common humanity.

So, the cost of corruption is not merely about lost money or poor governance. It comes at a price of shattered dreams, lost opportunities, eroded trust, and a bruised country. The cost is paid by the citizen, the society, and the future. It is carried by each decent human being who seeks to earn an honest living in dignity, by each child who is denied good education, by each family who loses a beloved one as a result of medical neglect, and by each human being who bears the pain of injustice yet remains voiceless.

In the words of Mahatma Gandhi, "A nation's greatness lies in the purity of its heart, the strength of its character, and the righteousness of its actions." When corruption runs rampant, that greatness is silently sold off—piece by piece, bribe by bribe. Retrieving it takes more than legislation—it takes courage, conscience, and the commitment to create a society in which justice cannot be bought.

# IV

# The Cultural and Political Economy of Corruption

Corruption does not exist in a vacuum; it finds nourishment in the soil of culture and the framework of political economy. It takes root in the values, norms, expectations, and fears of a society. When we start to view bribes not as violations of ethics but as a charge for service, or we justify nepotism as a matter of culture, corruption ceases to be the exception and becomes a norm. It is important to recognize that corruption isn't so much about broken systems—it's about broken mindsets, formed over decades by the way politics is organized, how institutions work, and how society rationalizes power and privilege.

In most parts of the globe, particularly in post-colonial nations like India, corruption is rationalized as a way of survival or advancement. Colonial administration bequeathed extractive institutions that valued conformity over accountability, hierarchy over justice. These institutions, even after independence, were not typically disassembled. Rather, they were reassigned to support new elites. The colonial bureaucracy, inherited mostly in its previous form, was never reoriented to be citizen-focused. Public service consequently continued to be a site of control and patronage and not empowerment and transparency.

The corruption political economy, particularly in democracies, is deeply interdependent with the organization of election politics. Political parties, based on enormous unaccounted resources to fight elections, tend to rely on illegal sources of funds. Cronyism is then a transactional imperative, in which contributions to campaigns purchase post-election influence. Politicians who are genuinely well-intentioned, bound by the compulsions of vote-bank politics, end up being sucked into the same game. It becomes a circle of violence: money purchases influence, and influence guards money. The political economist Pranab Bardhan has written of corruption in the developing world as a "functional necessity" of the system—a decentralized redistribution network that serves to keep the wheels of the political machine grease in the lack of transparent institutional financing.

At the cultural level, corruption also gets moral legitimacy through deeply embedded concepts of loyalty, family, and duty. In cultures where family or community is viewed as being more important than the state, public office itself is frequently treated as a means of advancing one's own kind rather than working for the good of the people. Hiring a relative, favoring friends, or getting employment for caste members is not typically viewed as immoral, but rather as doing one's social responsibility. This conflict between ancient duties and contemporary institutional principles is at the core of what sociologists such as André Béteille have characterized as the "dissonance of Indian modernity"—in which democratic values go alongside feudal culture.

Religion has also been a paradoxical influence on how people think about corruption. To the extent that most religious traditions inculcate the values of honesty, sympathy, and fairness, religion seems to encourage virtuous behavior rather than corruption. On the contrary, religion has at times been invoked to legitimize power structures and justify inequality. When wealth accumulation, regardless of means, is divine reward or karmic entitlement, corruption ceases to have a moral taint. Temples, ashrams, and religious institutions have themselves been involved in major financial scandals, revealing the intricate interplay of faith, money, and power. The works of Swami Vivekananda present, however, a starkly contrasting moral vision. He insisted on not ritualism but ethics, service, and the culture of selflessness—values that, if strictly adhered to, have no space for corruption.

The media, though widely credited as the fourth pillar of democracy, have also become a stakeholder in the political economy of corruption. Large corporate media conglomerates, reliant on government advertisements and corporate sponsorships, are frequently involved in muzzling or spinning corruption stories. Investigative journalism thrives more in the periphery—done by independent voices who are often harassed or silenced. Commercialization of news, the proliferation of paid media, and the weaponization of false narratives have all watered down the watchdog role of journalism. As Noam Chomsky also famously noted, when the media turns into a manufacturing consent mechanism instead of telling the truth to power, then democracy itself becomes a show with no substance.

Another significant phenomenon is the normalizing of aspirational consumerism in neoliberal economies. With liberalization of economics, material prosperity became the principal yardstick to measure self-worth. Advertisements, films, and social media keep perpetuating the notion that a person's worth is measured by the vehicle one drives, the label one wears, or the devices one possesses. This constant drive towards acquisition provides fertile soil for corrupt practices. When society worships wealth but does not inquire about its source, corruption becomes unseen—or better yet, admirable. Indian sociologist Ashis Nandy cautioned against this "banality of evil," whereby wrongdoings become so entrenched and socially condoned that they stop being offensive.

The education system, which should be the guard against moral deterioration, often turns complicit in the same culture that it needs to subvert. From private colleges paying capitation fees to leaked examination papers and nepotism in appointment to academics, the same institutions charged with instilling integrity are themselves stained. Youth entering the job market, already conditioned within this setting, are subtly instructed that honesty is idealistic rather than practical. The distance between the professed values and the lived norms is so great that it engenders a silent despair—and ultimately, a resigned complicity.

Corruption also flourishes when civic institutions are feeble. Low civic literacy levels, weak grievance redressal, and denial of legal aid ensure that the majority of citizens lack both the tools and the time to contest the system. Civil society groups, once key in mobilizing the marginalized, are more and more restrained—subjected to legal regulation, monitoring, and de-financing. Narrowing civic space undermines collective protest and enables corruption to spread unrestrained.

However, amidst all this, the cultural environment is not uniform. There are islands of opposition, usually by grassroots activists, whistleblowers, and reformist bureaucrats. Campaigns such as the Right to Information (RTI), initiated by Aruna Roy and the Mazdoor Kisan Shakti Sangathan, have demonstrated that citizen oversight can indeed unsettle the foundations of secretive governance. The effectiveness of such initiatives, however, rests on the availability of robust institutional support—enforced laws, responsive courts, and fearless media.

In conclusion, the political economy and culture of corruption cannot be separated from the society which nurtures it. It does not suffice to enact legislation or establish anti-corruption commissions. Unless we rethink our political financing, reform our public institutions, and redefine our societal values, corruption will keep mutating, adapting, and thriving. It is not just about punishing the corrupt—it is about building a culture where honesty is not heroic but normal. A culture where public service is a privilege, not a business opportunity. A culture where power is accountable, and where conscience is louder than convenience.

As Indian philosopher J Krishnamurti once said, "It is no measure of health to be well-adjusted to a profoundly sick society." In order to eliminate corruption, we need to cure the sickness at its cultural and political root—rebuild the soul of our institutions and the conscience of our collective being rather than treating symptoms.

## 4.1 Cultural Conditioning: Is Bribery Taught or Caught?

The question of whether bribery is consciously taught or subconsciously caught is at the center of how corruption becomes embedded in society. Although there exists no curriculum nor parenting manual advocating dishonesty openly, societies do pass on behavior through a silent pedagogy—a collection of unwritten lessons learned through observation, adaptation, and survival. Bribery, as social behavior, is seldom taught by direct instruction. It is learned, inferred, and legitimized through the day-to-day experiences of growing up in a morally ambiguous world.

Children observe and learn. A parent pays a traffic policeman and says to the child, "It's faster this way." A teacher is bribed to pad exam scores, and the student learns that competence can be circumvented. A contractor makes a 'cut' to a municipal official for quicker approval, and the society celebrates the project speed, not the method. These micro-moments of compromise get ingrained in the minds of the young. What is perceived as a short-term strategy becomes a lifelong tactic. In this way, bribery is not learned by doctrine but learned by social demonstration.

Sociologist M.N. Srinivas's "social mobility through sanskritization" identified the way in which marginalized groups pursued status by copying the practice of higher castes. Likewise, in corruption, the lower echelons of society tend to watch and imitate the informal methods of the hegemonic. When the powers-that-be get away with bending the rules, it sends the message down: rule-breaking is not a crime but an art, a capability that requires mastering if one is to thrive. This ingrains itself as part of cultural conditioning in the long run.

Bribery is also usually couched in the language of necessity. One bribes not because one desires to but because "the system leaves no choice." Whether it is securing a hospital bed, a school seat, or a pension file, individuals find that greasing palms is the most effective—sometimes the sole—means of getting things done. The institutionalization of this helplessness conditions attitudes. When millions practice bribery as civic survival, the act itself becomes depoliticized. It becomes routine, expected, even justified.

Philosopher Amartya Sen has written extensively about how freedom is not merely the absence of coercion but the presence of substantive choices. A society where citizens are coerced into corruption due to systemic bottlenecks cannot claim to be free in any meaningful sense. Individuals in such systems might not sanction bribery but engage in it, not with ill will but through adaptation. Corruption thus becomes learned helplessness, a means of coping with a Byzantine structure that defies openness.

Interestingly, cultural scripts regarding bribery vary by context. In certain communities, bribery is publicly denounced in religious sermons but secretly tolerated in family transactions. In others, it is perceived as cunningness—a showcase of street-smart haggling. Indian cinema has played a two-edged role here. On the one hand, movies have underscored the ills of corruption through tragic heroes and satiric stories. On the other, they have fantasized the 'fixer' figure—the antihero who manipulates the system to win. Such portrayals do not merely represent reality; they construct it.

Even language conforms to this conditioning. Euphemisms are plentiful—"chai-paani" (tea-water), "setting," "adjustment," or "token of appreciation." These verbal softeners render corruption as benign, even hospitable. When bribery is disguised as hospitality or a cultural gesture, it escapes ethical criticism. As Pierre Bourdieu implied, cultural capital exercises a powerful force in sanctioning practices that would otherwise appear suspect. When society embeds unethical behavior in its cultural grammar, resistance is hard.

In addition, socialization into corruption also involves the intersection with class and gender. Women, poor communities, and minority groups are more at risk of extortion but less likely to use bribery for gain. The privilege of paying bribes to become powerful is distinguishable from the vulnerability of being forced to pay bribes to stay alive. This difference tends to get lost in cultural accounts, which have a tendency to frame bribery as a symmetrical action instead of an expression of asymmetrical power relations.

In the end, whether bribery is caught or taught is not an either-or proposition—it is both. It is taught by implicit sanction, silence, and reward. It is caught by repetition, observation, and imitation. It persists not because human beings are by nature unscrupulous but because systems are by nature permissive and cultures are not self-critical enough. To break it, we need more than legal sanctions, and we need cultural change. We need to learn—and more crucially, to demonstrate—that honesty is not gullibility and that equity does not have to be an exception.

As Dr. B.R. Ambedkar rightly pointed out, "Cultivation of mind should be the ultimate aim of human existence." If we are to eradicate corruption, we need to cultivate minds that are capable of distinguishing right from the expedient, justice from convenience, and courage from compromise. It's then that we can dream of bringing up a generation that resists and does not replicate what it observes—and sets about creating a future free from the culture of bribery.

## 4.2 Politics of Patronage and Electoral Financing

The intersection of political patronage and electoral finance is at the center of institutional corruption. As opposed to petty bribery, which targets individuals at the periphery, political corruption infects the very center of democratic government. It distorts the ideals of representation, misshapes public policy, and corrupts the moral fabric of the state. In a nation such as India, in which democracy is regarded as a great experiment in popular will, the corrosive influence of patronage politics is usually overlooked—not because it is imperceptible, but because it has tragically become routine.

Patronage, in its classical connotation, means the dispensation of favors—appointments, contracts, access, protection—in exchange for political allegiance. In a more nefarious guise, it is a system in which public funds are traded for votes, favors, or campaign contributions. This clientelist system is not outside of the state but internal to its everyday operations. Political functionaries, particularly in state and local hierarchies, are reduced to dispensers of favors, not as a matter of their constitutional function but because of the electoral compulsions that require them to deliver palpably to the constituency—usually at the expense of legality or competence.

Election finance is the lifeblood of this process. Indian politics is an increasingly costly business, with the costs of mobilization of masses, outreach through the media, event organization, and social media manipulation going through the roof. The Election Commission of India sets a limit on official expenditure by candidates, but in practice, actual expenditure typically far outstrips legal bounds. The deficiency is filled up with murky, unaccounted money—informally known as 'black money'—injected in by corporates, contractors, lobbies, and rent-seekers. The money is hardly ever provided gratis; it is an investment expecting returns in terms of contracts, licenses, policy adjustments, or exemption from regulation.

Dr. Pranab Bardhan, India's most renowned political economist, has long maintained that corruption in developing nations is not a failure of moral character but a structural aspect of the organization and reward of power. In his view, the relationship between political parties and business elites produces an "institutional equilibrium" in which all—bureaucrats, politicians, industrialists—have an interest in preserving the existing order. In such a system, corruption is not an aberration; it is the operating principle.

Political finance, in such a scenario, becomes both a cause and an effect of corruption. Politicians need money to win elections that is not possible through legal sources alone. Once in power, they indulge in rent-seeking activity to get returns on their investment. Government orders, public properties, mining licenses, infrastructure works, and even welfare programs turn into instruments of extraction. Power is used to accumulate wealth and wealth to perpetuate power in a self-generating system.

The introduction of Electoral Bonds in India was intended to introduce a degree of transparency to political contributions. Yet, critics have argued that the bonds, although legal, cannot be traced back to the public, enabling companies and individuals to contribute to parties anonymously. The Association for Democratic Reforms (ADR) has also pointed out how most of these funds have disproportionately accrued to the ruling party, raising questions about the competitive neutrality and fairness of elections. When money is the single determining factor in politics, democracy starts looking more like an auction than a choice.

Patronage politics also gets enacted across social and identity lines. Caste, religion, and regional identity are tended to not merely for ideological resonance but as patronage constituencies. Political bosses offer specific benefits—reservations, subsidies, loan waivers, or symbolic status—in exchange for electoral support. Social scientist Rajni Kothari referred to this as the "politics of caste and clientelism," where democratic representation is a game of selective appeasement and not universal inclusion. In such a scenario, public goods are no longer delivered on the basis of need or efficiency but based on the ability of a group to mobilize political influence.

In addition, patronage networks drain the state from within. Appointments, transfers, and promotions in the bureaucracy become politicized. Policemen, tax officials, district collectors, and engineers are regularly changed to suit political considerations. This erodes institutional autonomy, dilutes accountability, and promotes a culture of loyalty to the ruling party over adherence to the Constitution.

As political philosopher Noam Chomsky has noted in American politics, "The smart way to keep people passive and obedient is to strictly limit the spectrum of acceptable opinion, but allow very lively debate within that spectrum." India as well sees the theater of democratic debate overlook the deeper accord binding all large political parties—a mutual reliance on inscrutable funding and patronage networks. The difference lies not in the approach, but in the rhetoric.

The real expense of this network is paid for by the citizen. Public goods are compromised, merit is by-passed, inequality is enhanced, and cynicism takes over from trust. When a system pays off favors rather than skills, and acquiescence instead of scrutiny, it undermines the very essence of citizenship. Elections become sporadic rituals of support instead of instruments of accountability.

To confront such a system demands more than reforms; it calls for a change in political culture. Public financing of campaigns, stricter laws on corporate contributions, independent auditing of political funds, and increased oversight by civil society are steps needed—but inadequate. What ultimately is needed is a shared moral awakening that views political office as public trust rather than as a business investment.

In the words of Mahatma Gandhi, "The best politics is right action." Until politics regains the ethics of public service, and until finance becomes accountable and transparent, the vicious cycle of corruption and patronage will continue to hold the state in chains of its own creation.

### 4.3 Media, Silence, and Manufactured Consent

The media, much touted as the fourth pillar of democracy, wields an enormous power to shape public awareness. In a democratic society, it fulfills not only the role of conveying information but questioning power, giving voice to the underprivileged, and playing the watchdog for abuse. Yet in most instances—particularly in the sphere of political corruption—this exemplary institution has fallen short of its ideals. The media's silence, and sometimes its collusion, does not only assist in the naturalization of corruption but in the construction of public consent for a system thatfeeds on dishonesty, opaqueness, and selective indignation.

The term "manufactured consent," used by political theorist Edward S. Herman and linguist-philosopher Noam Chomsky, is used to describe the way in which dominant institutions create public opinion by controlling mass communication. Although Chomsky initially used the term to describe Western democracies, its application to postcolonial democracies such as India is becoming increasingly obvious. In a corporate-and-political-driven media environment, news becomes a product designed not for truth but for consumption—designed to perpetuate the status quo.

The issue is not one of bias or sensationalism. It is more fundamental—a systemic habit of omission, in which certain truths are smothered beneath a flood of trivia. When a prominent politician is accused of corruption, when a big financial scandal is uncovered, or when systematic abuses are revealed, media reaction usually follows a predictable pattern: initial outrage, superficial debate, and then sudden silence. What should have given rise to continued investigative reporting and public mobilization is instead replaced by distraction—gossip about celebrities, religious polarisation, or jingoistic hysteria.

The silence is calculated. Most of the big media outlets are controlled by corporate conglomerates whose business empires are inextricably linked to political patronage. Investigative reporting on corruption therefore becomes a financial risk. Advertising revenue, regulatory clearances, land licenses, and tax scrutiny all become instruments through which governments can reward or punish the media. Under such a scenario, journalism is quietly converted into public relations, and editors turn into risk managers instead of truth seekers.

Veteran Indian journalist P. Sainath, who has been feared for his steadfast attention to rural poverty and government failure, once wrote, "The media in India is not failing. It is succeeding brilliantly at doing what it is designed to do: distract, divide, and pacify." This perceptive commentary speaks not to journalistic incompetence, but to a far more sinister trend—the intentional design of distraction. Reporting on corruption is frequently boiled down to sensationalized arguments on late-night TV, in which real issues are overwhelmed by noise, and substance is substituted with spectacle.

In addition, social media has not necessarily made information more democratic. While it provides room for opposition voices and independent reporting, it also facilitates the quick dissemination of misinformation. Troll armies, bot networks, and organized campaigns blur the distinction between fact and fiction. Whistleblowers are demonized, critics labeled as "anti-national," and actual issues are smothered in a tsunami of manufactured narratives. The very tools that could have facilitated scrutiny by the public are now used to manufacture consent for the elite.

Media complicity in corruption is not only in what it conceals—it is also in what it normalizes. Ongoing reporting of corruption cases that never come to fruition results in public exhaustion and disinterest. Human beings convince themselves that politicians are all corrupt, systems all broken, and nothing can be done to alter them. Such cynical resignation benefits the corrupt, who function most effectively when the people assume nothing. Under such an atmosphere, even sincere reforms are greeted with distrust, and real dissent is smothered by skepticism.

It should be kept in mind that silence is never neutrality. Under social injustice and political corruption, silence tends to mean approval. As philosopher Hannah Arendt cautioned, "The greatest evil is not radical, it is the evil of banality." When the media normalizes corruption, when it shies away from inconvenient facts, and when it makes false comparisons, it does not only fall short of its responsibility—it is an accomplice to institutional rot.

Of course, there are exceptions. Free digital platforms, freelance reporters, and citizen-run initiatives still fight the spirit of journalism against stiff opposition. From Ravish Kumar's unapologetic news reads to the pioneering investigations of sites like The Wire, Scroll, and Alt News, there are indeed spaces of resistance. But these are silenced by trollers, intimidators, economically strangled. Space for autonomous inquiry is vanishing, along with the popular imagination of public life without corruption.

Finally, a democratic society needs an educated citizenry, and an educated citizenry cannot be had without a courageous and ethical media. The question is not whether the press reports corruption, but whether it derrides the systems which enable corruption to thrive. Until journalism regains its watchdog role and tears off the masks of servility and sensationalism, the corruption will continue to be legitimized in the shadows.

### 4.4 Corruption as a Class Tool: The Poor vs the Protected

Corruption is usually debated as a moral failure, a transgression against rules, or an institutional lapse in ethics. However, such debates hardly ever challenge a deeper reality: corruption is not equally impactful on all people. It is neither class-less nor system-less. In reality, corruption is a class tool—an unseen, subtle system that penalizes the poor for staying alive while shielding the privileged as they plunder. It maintains hierarchy in the name of opportunity and enforces inequality in the name of governance.

For the economically disadvantaged, corruption is not a newspaper headline—it is a way of life. A poor woman applying for a ration card has to bribe the local official. A daily-wage laborer injured at work may need to grease palms to access basic healthcare. A farmer trying to register land has to navigate a maze of clerks, middlemen, and opaque forms, each extractive. In such contexts, corruption is not simply transactional; it becomes existential. It dictates whether one eats, learns, heals, or survives.

Contrast this with the corruption that serves the rich—the protected. Among the elite, corruption is redescribed as lobbying, influence, or "relationship management." Regulatory capture, policy niceness adjustments, and sweet deals are wrapped in legalize and legitimated as economic prudence. When a billionaire defaults on a loan, it's "NPAs" and written off as a systemic problem; when a poor peasant defaults, it's criminalized, and usually ends in suicide. As economist Prabhat Patnaik has always maintained, the state under a neoliberal regime turns into the guardian of capital, not of the people—a broker for the wealthy rather than a defender of the weak.

The Indian sociologist Gopal Guru once wrote that the corruption narrative itself is elitist. It positions the bribe-taker as morally corrupt while excluding the structural imbalances that compel the poor to get involved in corrupt systems just to gain access to their rights. The upper classes, on the other hand, practice legal corruption—using tax havens, obtaining favorable verdicts, or manipulating land purchases—under the cover of institutional respectability. Their corruption is seldom punished and frequently rewarded.

This class inequality is also apparent in the manner in which laws are enforced. Anti-corruption campaigns disproportionately victimize minor government officials—clerks, traffic police, junior officers—while big-time embezzlers and political fundraisers are left untouched. The over-exposure of the lower levels of the bureaucracy makes it possible for higher levels to go scot-free. The performance of reform therefore hides the preservation of privilege.

It is also revealing the way surveillance technologies and digitization of welfare tend to heighten surveillance over the poor while protecting the rich. The poor are repeatedly required to establish their entitlement—Aadhaar-linked ration, biometric attendance, income certificates—while the rich are assumed to be in compliance until they are caught. This is design corruption, where the systems themselves are biased against the powerless. Philosopher Ambedkar cautioned that any democracy that fails to deal with social and economic inequality is only a sham. If the poor have to pay to receive the bare minimum while the wealthy are given the maximum for free, then corruption is not only an aberration—it is the defining characteristic of a grossly unequal state.

In addition, the story that makes the poor "beneficiaries" and the wealthy "wealth creators" doubles the injustice. Welfare is viewed as a tax burden, yet tax evasion by big business is viewed as an economic imperative. This ideological sleight of hand enables the actual corrupt—the ones stealing resources on a massive scale—to wear suits and get awards, while the poor are demonized for being 'too dependent' or 'undeserving'.

In rural settings, corruption frequently overlaps with caste and thus becomes a double instrument of class and social oppression. Lower-caste communities, such as Dalits and Adivasis, are not only subject to administrative obstacles but social discrimination when accessing public services. Corruption in these places is not merely monetary—it is a matter of denial, exclusion, and humiliation. Their rights become favors, dependent on appeasing local elites, party workers, or bureaucratic go-betweens.

This cycle is repeated all over the world. Everywhere in the world, the poor are criminalized for operating within dirty systems, and the wealthy devise new ways to launder influence and legitimacy. International financial institutions talk of "good governance," but frequently bankroll regimes that safeguard investor interest at the expense of citizen dignity. As Thomas Piketty has demonstrated, the concentration of capital is frequently sustained through political complicity and policy manipulation, facilitated by corruption that is legal, institutional, and unseen.

The discourse on corruption must thus be moved away from morality to materiality—from personal sin to structural criticism. Who benefits? Who loses? Who is shielded and who is penalized? These are the questions that actually matter. Until we accept that corruption is a tool of class domination, efforts at reform will remain cosmetic, addressing the symptoms while shielding the illness.

In the end, corruption is not a leveler; it is a divider. It widens the gap between the haves and the have-nots, makes exploitation legitimate, and strengthens a system in which survival for the poor hinges on silence, and impunity for the elite is masqueraded as competence. If corruption is a game, the poor never even get the rules—let alone the dice.

### 4.5 Can Religion and Ethics Save Us?

The promise of religion and ethics has always been to keep human greed, pride, and injustice in check. From ancient texts to contemporary sermons, from village priests to university philosophers, the exhortation has been one: "Do unto others as you would have them do unto you." And yet, the ubiquity of corruption—after two millennia of ethical exhortation—poses a deep and discomfiting question: Can ethics and religion save us from corruption, or have they themselves become accomplices, wittingly or not?

Religions throughout the world, such as Hinduism, Islam, Christianity, Buddhism, and Sikhism, condemn dishonesty, exploitation, and injustice. The Bhagavad Gita refers to dharma—the right path—as core to one's duty. Islam requires justice (adl) and forbids rishwa (bribery). Christianity warns of loving money as the "root of all evil," and Buddhism points to the Eightfold Path that involves right action and right livelihood. These values, at face value, must make corruption morally indefensible.

And yet, religious communities—both Eastern and Western—are not above corruption; some are actually filled with it. How does one account for this contradiction? Philosopher Amartya Sen once said that morality cannot be outsourced to institutions or traditions—it must be critically scrutinized and internally assimilated. Religion, in this sense, can offer a vocabulary for ethics, but not its automatic implementation.

In India, religion is inextricably a part of everyday life, but there are scams with religious charities, temple trusts, and gurus galore. The irony is stark: the same organizations that preach truth and plain living harbor powerbrokers and money launderers at times. The commercialization of faith—donations as deals, blessings as products, and rituals as premium-priced ones—erodes the moral authority of religion. It turns the sacred into a marketplace, making faith complicit in the very corruption it condemns.

Ethics, as philosophically taught, has not done so badly. Philosophers such as M.K. Gandhi demanded that the ends should never justify the means. His Satyagraha philosophy was built on strict adherence to truth even in the most adverse of situations. However, in the pragmatic politics of contemporary government and commerce, Gandhian ethics is derided as idealistic or unrealistic. Once results matter more than morality, and profit takes precedence over principle, ethics takes a backseat.

Nevertheless, ethics has one conclusive advantage over religious dogma: the potential to be secular, dynamic, and responsive to shifting contexts. Rabindranath Tagore, profoundly religious but questioning of organized religion, was of the opinion that ethical awareness must be born out of inner freedom rather than fear of punishment or promise of reward. He saw morality as not commandment, but awakening—a blossoming of one's higher self. That perspective opens a critical space where ethics can be cultivated through education, debate, and democratic participation, rather than inherited unquestioningly.

Religion has usually had to depend on fear—fear of divine retribution or karmic payback—to curb corruption. Effective in certain situations, this so-called morality of fear is weak. When faith deters or loopholes find justification—like donations to temples in black money in return for public redemption—the moral brakes fail. Ethics, in contrast, is not foisted from above but self-imposed. It takes sensitivity, not compliance.

But can religion and ethics co-exist? Maybe. If read carefully, critically, and not as dogma, religion can support ethical action by placing it within a grand cosmic or communal scheme. It can spur selflessness, empathy, and bravery. Many whistleblowers and reformers—from Vinoba Bhave to Anna Hazare—have derived strength from religious belief to push back against institutional rot. Religion, in these cases, functions as a moral agency instead of a ritualistic formalism.

Sociologist André Béteille pointed out that India's moral issue is not a deficiency of moral language, but a surfeit of moral hypocrisy. Individuals talk of virtue in public but practice it in private. Ethics turns into performance, not practice. The problem, thus, is not the lack of moral frameworks, but their selective use. Religion and ethics need to be brought into congruence with action in everyday life, not separated from it.

So can religion and ethics save us? Not by themselves. They need to be combined with political will, legal reform, education of the civic sphere, and institutional responsibility. Religion can move us, but not pass laws. Ethics can inform us, but not mandate. To see them as saviors is to put too much faith in individual morality in a world designed by structural inequality and power dynamics.

And yet we should not forsake them, either. During an era of cynicism, when corruption has seemed to settle in, religion and ethics are a vocabulary of hope. They speak to us of the fact that integrity remains, that values count. Their strength is not in sermons or rituals but in action—day-by-day decisions by everyday people who will act right when it is hard.

Finally, religion and ethics can't save us until we save them first—save them from hypocrisy, from commodification, from political manipulation. Only then can they become the moral compass we so desperately require.

# V

# Rethinking Reform – Can We De-Normalize Corruption?

Corruption, which was once seen as an aberration from the norm, has become the norm itself in most societies. It no longer surprises; it only irritates. From the bribes for everyday services to the big-ticket embezzlement of public money in multi-crore scams, corruption has integrated itself into the rhythm of everyday life. The actual threat, though, is not merely its frequency, but its normalization—the unspoken social covenant embracing it as unavoidable. Redoing reform, thus, is not merely about transforming systems or legislations, but about learning to un-accept and re-moralizing imagination. The task at hand is a pressing one: is it possible to de-normalize corruption?

To even start such a process, we have to face the unpleasant reality that reform attempts till now have tended to be cosmetic. Legislation has been passed, institutions established, and investigations launched—but the underlying ethos hasn't changed. Indian economist and ex-RBI Governor Dr. Raghuram Rajan rightly noted that "bad economics makes good politics." This perverse logic tends to fuel populist choices that cover up structural rot. Anti-corruption agencies are not independent, watchdog organizations are under-resourced, and the judiciary labors under a pendency. The state appears trapped in a cycle of superficial cleansing and quiet perpetuation.

Reform, if it is to be authentic, has to start by disavowing this fatalism. Corruption feeds not only on loopholes but also on reduced expectations. Citizens do not ask for better governance because they have stopped believing that it can be delivered. Philosopher Antonio Gramsci would refer to this as a type of "cultural hegemony"—where the prevailing worldview (in this instance, that 'everyone is corrupt') becomes internalized by rulers and ruled alike. Under such an environment, even the honest are bullied into the corrupt system in order to survive. De-normalizing corruption involves shattering this hegemony—shifting resignation to resistance, and cynicism to civic hope.

This hope has to be cultivated through civic literacy and ethical reorientation. Reform has to reach not only institutions but consciousness. That is where teachers, artists, public intellectuals, and youth movements become important. Reforms based solely on policy tend to collapse because they don't engage with the cultural soil on which corruption takes root. A society that starts questioning, debating, and ridiculing corruption, however, can start delegitimizing it. Corruption lives in silence. It withers under scrutiny.

An essential tactic in this war is openness—not as a buzzword but as a principle lived. Right to Information (RTI) law was such an effort, making citizens agents to cut through the shroud of bureaucratic secrecy. Even that tool, though, is facing danger, with mounting attacks on RTI activists and mounting bureaucratic resistance. Openness must be protected and amplified—not merely in government but also in corporates, NGOs, and media. As economist Jean Drèze points out, "Transparency is not a silver bullet, but without it, nothing else works." Once citizens understand how decisions are being made, who gains, and who loses, they are able to confront the machinery of impunity.

Systemic transparency, however, has to be accompanied by strong accountability. Bureaucrats and politicians implicated in acts of corruption never see real consequences. Either cases linger on interminably or punishments are token. This impunity sends a message to others that corruption is not only acceptable—it is, in fact, risk-free. This has to change. Accountability has to be prompt, equal, and transparent. Citizens have to notice that the state is not only committed to punishing the corrupt but also to safeguarding the honest. Whistleblower protection legislation has to be made stronger, not weaker.

Another of the pillars of reform is decentralization. If power is too centralized, corruption is more efficient and less easy to oppose. Local government, if well equipped and empowered, can allow people to monitor development at first hand. Methods such as participatory budgeting, social audits, and report cards have been effective in states such as Kerala and Rajasthan. These are not instruments—these are democratic routines that incrementally de-normalize corruption by engaging individuals in their own administration.

But reforms will amount to nothing if they fail to address the economic causes of corruption. When jobs in the public sector are limited, welfare is porous, and inequality is rampant, corruption tends to become a survival strategy. Moral policing is not the answer but economic equity. Providing decent employment, investment in public infrastructure, and curbing discretionary powers of bureaucrats can eliminate the incentives that make corruption appealing. As Dr. B.R. Ambedkar cautioned, political democracy cannot coexist with social and economic democracy. Reform must tackle both.

Notably, we also need to challenge the vocabulary we apply to corruption. Too often, it is talked about in the language of "loss to the exchequer" or "harm to the economy." True, but such a definition makes corruption an economic abstraction removed from the real lives of the poor. Corruption kills. It denies citizens medicine, rationing, shelter, and justice. It should be identified as a human rights violation. When we start perceiving corruption as not merely economic inefficiency but social brutality, the necessity of reform becomes moral, rather than managerial.

To de-normalize corruption, reform cannot be episodic—it must be cultural. The goal is not merely to punish the corrupt, but to make corruption unacceptable. This transformation will take time, but history offers hope. Practices like untouchability, once normalized, were eventually challenged and stigmatized. Norms do change when societies evolve in moral consciousness.

Finally, reform is not a to-do list—it's a movement. It needs students, writers, street vendors, judges, poets, and panchayat leaders. It needs to go from textbooks to TV debates, from Twitter to street corners. It needs to make the honest less lonely and the corrupt less confident. De-normalizing corruption involves re-humanizing our public life—rebuilding trust, empathy, and the faith that honesty is not frailty but vigor.

We may not eradicate corruption completely. But we can make it more difficult. We can make it shameful. We can make it risky. We begin the process of reform when citizens stop murmuring about corruption and begin to shout about justice.

### 5.1 Why Most Anti-Corruption Campaigns Fail

The path to reform is usually lined with good intentions, but in the world of anti-corruption, these intentions seldom lead to change that lasts. Around the world, there have been countless campaigns that have vowed to purify the system, but corruption persists, evolving and changing like a virus. The causes of these failures lie not so much in the power of corruption, but in the frailty—both structural and psychological—of the campaigns mounted against it. Closer scrutiny indicates that the majority of anti-corruption initiatives fail because they attack symptoms, not systems; people, not ideologies; legality, not legitimacy.

One of the primary reasons for the failure of anti-corruption campaigns is their narrow emphasis on criminality and not complicity. They approach corruption as a series of criminal actions by nefarious individuals, and not as a matrix of systemic inducements that push even the good towards compromise. Legislation is strengthened, inspectors are named, and investigations are initiated—though these may superficially skimp the surface. As Indian economist Kaushik Basu noted during his stint as Chief Economic Adviser, most anti-corruption efforts overlook that in some situations, both bribe-taker and bribe-giver are corrupt and reasonable actors adjusting to institutional failure. Basu even suggested a provocative but brilliant concept: legalizing the giving of harassment bribes as a means of stimulating whistleblowing and shattering the code of silence. His suggestion illustrates how conventional legal frameworks often fail to capture the complexity of real-world corruption.

Another reason campaigns fail is their over-reliance on symbolism over substance. Political regimes frequently weaponize anti-corruption rhetoric as a tool of moral superiority, branding opponents as corrupt while turning a blind eye to their own misdemeanors. This creates a selective enforcement regime where justice appears partisan. The public quickly loses faith. Anti-corruption becomes drama—a spectacle that has little structural impact. This selective ethics weakens not just the credibility of the campaign but also hardens cynicism amongst citizens, who come to read such drives as moments of political score-settling rather than attempts at substantive reform.

Most often, too, the institutional framework intended to combat corruption is itself corrupted. Anti-corruption agencies usually are not independent, and ombudsman offices are poorly funded or politically silenced. In India, the eagerly awaited Lokpal Act established a statutory agency to probe corruption at the top, but its implementation has been glacially slow. Without teeth, even laws well-drafted remain decorative. As Indian sociologist Ghanshyam Shah noted, unless institutions are insulated from political meddling and vested with actual sanctioning powers, they cannot function as effective checks on abuse of power.

No less problematic is the technocratic nature of most anti-corruption initiatives. While digitization, biometric IDs, and blockchain technologies are hopeful tools, they are not panaceas. They can reduce transactional corruption but cannot do away with systemic or political corruption. Worse still, without simultaneous human reforms—ethical training, transparency norms, and civic education—technology can merely automate current biases or be evaded altogether. As economist Jean Drèze cautions, "Technology can be a powerful ally of the people—but only if people are organized to use it." Without people, however, technology remains a shiny imposter for justice.

Anti-corruption crusades also falter when they fail to take account of the culturalterrain on which corruption germinates. In cultures where corruption seeps into the fabric of daily life—school admissions, hospital beds—blanket appeals to "be honest" ring insincere. Bribery, cronyism, and jugaad are not aberrations but survival techniques. Without tackling the socio-economic insecurities that compel people to indulge in them, demands for probity sound hollow. Reform has to begin with empathy rather than censure. Thinker M.N. Roy adhered to the principle that ethical reconstruction should follow political change, lest the latter becomes theatrics. Roy's observation is essential: change of morality cannot be ordered but needs to be nurtured.

Also, most campaigns do not have sustained public participation. They burst forth as a reaction to scandals or crises, but subside without continued citizen involvement. The India Against Corruption movement in 2011 rallied millions, but lost its momentum to electoral politics and internal disintegration. Public passion was not translated into institutional reform. Anti-corruption, to be effective, has to be a people's movement—not merely a bureaucratic order. It will need to create coalitions that cross class, caste, and region, generating grassroots vigilance and institutional change.

One must also acknowledge the psychological aspect of these failures. Most campaigns deploy shame and fear as drivers, casting corruption as a moral cancer. But behavioural economics demonstrates that guilt alone is a poor deterrent, particularly where the social setting legitimises the act. More powerful, though, is the transformation of default norms—turning transparency into the rule, rather than the exception. That takes patient, incremental efforts in education, the media, family life, and even in religious instruction. Development, writes Amartya Sen, is not just about growing economies; it is about broadening freedom and capabilities as much as GDP. A community that produces free, inquiring, and ethically informed people will be more resistant to corruption than one that just passes punishing legislation.

Finally, anti-corruption campaigns tend to underestimate the international scale of corruption. Illicit financial flows, tax havens, and multinational lobbying create a transnational environment that harbors and rewards corruption. National initiatives are defeated when international finance provides safe haven to the corrupt. Hence, anti-corruption also has to be an international agenda—an agenda that requires corporate accountability, financial transparency, and ethical globalization. Otherwise, we are only plugging holes in a sinking ship.

In total, most anti-corruption efforts fail because they are reactive, disjointed, and cosmetic. They try to catch the thief, but not uproot the culture of thievery. They punish but do not change. In order for reform to succeed, it has to be comprehensive—legal, ethical, institutional, and cultural. It has to start with truth, live on trust, and be fueled by public courage. Corruption cannot be shamed away; it needs to be redefined out of existence.

### 5.2 Lessons from Global Movements

The battle against corruption is neither new nor a uniquely regional or cultural problem. It is one that democracies and dictatorships have both contended with for centuries. Yet in the midst of these recurrent struggles, certain movements not only fought back against corruption but reimagined the structure of power. Theirs are stories of lessons—lessons in organizing, in moral clarity, in design of institutions, and most of all, in the potential of collective change.

One of the most legendary recent examples is likely to be Hong Kong's Anti-Corruption Revolution of the 1970s. This started as mass outrage at large-scale police bribery and ended with the establishment of the Independent Commission Against Corruption (ICAC)—now a model for study all over the world. What set the ICAC apart was that it had three branches: enforcement, prevention, and education for the community. The Commission was vested with unfettered autonomy, robust investigatory powers, and a clear mandate to inform citizens about ethics and integrity. In ten years, the petty-bribery culture that had pervaded all of Hong Kong's public life—hospital admissions, construction permits—plummeted. The lesson: sustained institutional independence and concurrent public engagement are essential. As ex-ICAC commissioner Bertrand de Speville rightly put it, "Anti-corruption reform that does not involve the people will eventually be reversed by the people."

Another compelling example is found in Scandinavian nations, Denmark and Sweden, regularly placed among the world's least corrupt countries. These countries did not achieve this status overnight, nor through deterrence based on fear. Rather, they have invested in long-term cultural and institutional development: social trust, transparent bureaucracy, generous welfare states, and equitable access to public services. Their public officials are among the world's best compensated, not as extravagance, but as protection against money temptations. Further, open data policies, citizens' right to information, and freedom of the press guarantee that power is under scrutiny at all times. The philosophical basis here is aligned with the reasoning of Amartya Sen, who was at pains to point out that democratic accountability is not merely a means of governance but also a ethical force which enriches people's capabilities and agency.

In Latin America, the Lava Jato (Operation Car Wash) debacle in Brazil at first seemed to be a shining beacon of accountability. It uncovered a huge web of kickbacks that involved the state-owned oil company Petrobras and senior political leaders. At its height, the operation jailed senior corporate leaders and even a former president. Although the operation was later criticized for its supposed politicization and procedural excesses, the initial popular backing it received showed how profound public desire for accountability is in a democracy weighed down by elite impunity. The rise and fall of Lava Jato teaches a vital lesson: anti-corruption efforts need to stay non-partisan and legally solid, lest they implode through their own contradictions.

Closer to us, India's 2011 India Against Corruption campaign, spearheaded by Anna Hazare, rekindled a moral awakening in the nation. Millions marched in the streets calling for the Lokpal (ombudsman) to battle high-level corruption. Briefly, civil society retook the republic's moral high ground. The movement was able to captivate national and international attention, pushing Parliament to adopt long-delays bills. But it also made visible the limitations of mobilization that focused on leaders. Without constant institutional follow-through, the movement disintegrated—part absorbed into electoral politics, part evaporated in civil exhaustion. The lasting lesson here is that moral energy has to be turned into systemic architecture; symbolism without structure is subject to co-option or decay.

Worldwide, we also have other creative grassroots models such as Participatory Budgeting in Porto Alegre, Brazil, where citizens themselves vote directly on the expenditure of public money in their own neighborhoods. This model, now duplicated in more than 1,500 cities around the world, is an experiment in democracy with transparency and local empowerment. By placing decision-making in the hands of citizens, it reduces the monopoly of bureaucrats and politicians over public money, thereby minimizing corruption at the source. Such initiatives embody what economist Elinor Ostrom advocated: that communities, when given real voice and autonomy, can manage resources more efficiently and equitably than centralized authorities.

In Africa, Kenya's Digital Governance Movement demonstrates how the technology can be used to limit discretion and obscurity. Kenya's e-procurement system (IFMIS) and electronic land registry have stifled routes for bribery and forgery. Likewise, Rwanda has adopted digitization and performance contracts to enhance state accountability. Critics, however, warn that technology has to be accompanied by political pluralism and civil freedoms; otherwise, it would turn into an instrument of control and not transparency.

Another motivating campaign is Transparency International, established in 1993 by a then-whistleblowing World Bank employee Peter Eigen, who became disenchanted with the organization's complicity in corruption by its silence. TI revolutionized the international anti-corruption narrative through the utilization of measures such as the Corruption Perceptions Index, compelling global institutions and governments to confront their integrity lapses. Transparency International's success is due to its dual strategy: creating a world-wide narrative while cultivating local chapters responsive to cultural contexts. It demonstrates that corruption is not only a national problem—it is a worldwide moral challenge needing networks of conscience and cooperation.

Notably, these international movements demonstrate that cultural transformation has to go hand in hand with institutional reform. As the philosopher Cornel West frequently puts it, "Justice is what love looks like in public." Anti-corruption, therefore, is not merely administrative purity—it is a moral endeavor of love for the common good, of not betraying the collective by succumbing to private greed.

What do these worldwide movements ultimately teach us? They teach us that combating corruption is not merely a question of punishing the corrupt. It is a matter of restructuring incentives, constructing institutions of trust, developing moral awareness, decentralizing power, and facilitating active citizenship. There is no one template, but there is a common philosophy: that a world more honest is not born—it is constructed, breath by breath, law by law, and deed by deed.

## 5.3 Education and Conscious Citizenship

At the core of any real and enduring reform is a much more profound force than punishing legislation or institutional plans: the forging of human consciousness. Education, when grounded in ethics and reflective thinking, becomes the most lasting instrument to create a citizenry that does not obey laws out of fear but enforces them out of conviction. It is in classrooms, homes, and the public sphere that societies inculcate the values which either normalize or abhor corruption. If corruption is a learned behavior—so much rooted in mimicry and silence as in system dysfunction—then education must be the moral counterbalance that instructs in resistance, integrity, and courage.

Throughout history, most of the world's great minds have emphasized the redemptive potential of education in creating not only good workers or knowledgeable voters, but morally enlightened individuals. Rabindranath Tagore, India's great philosopher-poet, felt that education must expand "the mind to think freely, the heart to feel deeply, and the will to act rightly." He had a vision of schools as holy places where the soul learns not only arithmetic and grammar, but the moral responsibility of being a human being towards others.

Similarly, Dr. B.R. Ambedkar, the mastermind behind the Indian Constitution, considered education to be the primary weapon against oppression and social degradation. "Cultivation of the mind should be the ultimate aim of human existence," he penned. For him, education was not merely an individual right but a shared tool to question hierarchies, challenge power, and seek justice—qualities that are vital for an anti-corruption culture.

In the modern day, education should change to cover moral reasoning, civic literacy, and critical awareness of the media. It does not suffice to have students memorize definitions of corruption; rather, they must be led to analyze why corruption succeeds, the ways in which it hides within euphemistic terms such as 'networking' or 'facilitation', and what the manifestations are of corruption in their everyday surroundings. For example, when a child sees his parents bribe someone to get ahead of a school admissions line or to avoid a traffic ticket, the unspoken lesson is that legality can be sacrificed for personal convenience. The work of education is to interrupt that chain—to provide children with words and power to label wrongdoing, even when it is socially sanctioned.

This lesson is where conscious citizenship is important. A thinking citizen is not an inactive consumer of services but a willing participant in governance. She/he queries, demands transparency, files RTIs (Right to Information), is present at public hearings, and most importantly, declines to acquiesce to petty acts of corruption, however socially convenient or economically advantageous it may be. As the philosopher J. Krishnamurti cautioned, "It is no measure of health to be well adjusted to a profoundly sick society." Conscious citizenship is, then, usually discomfiting—it shakes, challenges, and resists a culture of silence. But that very discomfiture is the mark of moral awakening.

Globally, initiatives such as service learning, model parliaments, and youth governance forums are promising to develop active, ethical young citizens. In India, initiatives such as 'Youth for Governance', civic-tech initiatives like I Change My City, or classroom activities under the CBSE's Value Education curriculum are early but significant steps in developing civic imagination.

Yet, a truly transformative education system must also confront structural inequalities. It can't teach morality in a society where there are students whose households are institutionally privileged and those who have to endure spaces in which gaming the system is considered the only road to dignity. That is the task of pedagogical justice—to not merely instruct students in compliance with norms but to encourage them to become aware of unfair rules and resist them, and to struggle to establish more just systems that curb the temptation and necessity to become corrupt.

Economist and philosopher Jean Drèze, in his research on education and development in India, has placed greater emphasis on the creation of what he refers to as "democratic practice" in daily school life. In schools where students vote for class representatives, debate social issues, and engage in decision-making, democratic culture is instilled early. These routines are the building blocks of an accountable adult citizenry.

Similarly, Paulo Freire, the Brazilian educator, also presented a strong argument for education that enhances critical consciousness or conscientização. He cautioned against traditional education tending to reproduce injustice by presenting students as passive recipients of knowledge. Rather, Freire advocated for dialogical education—where students become co-producers of knowledge, questioning the world around them. In these classrooms, the source of corruption—whether the offspring of apathy, fear, or blind obedience—may be brought to light and eradicated.

It is well worth recalling that even the best anti-corruption laws fail when used in a population that is illiterate about values. By contrast, even faulty systems can be defied by a people who possess robust moral compasses. Thus, education cannot be turned into mere vocational training or examination results. It has to aim higher—it has to construct citizens who can defy a bribe, challenge an unjust system, and bring power to account.

Finally, the issue is not whether education can rid us of corruption altogether—it can't. But it can sow the seeds of a world in which such tolerance no longer exists. It can educate a generation that doesn't roll its eyes in acceptance but stands instead in opposition. And in the process, it creates the only sort of democracy it's worth fighting for—not one in which people fear the law, but one in which honesty is valued.

### 5.4 Technology and Transparency: Double-Edged Sword

Technology's promise as an antidote to corruption has been welcomed by policymakers, technocrats, and activists alike with great hopefulness. Publicly digitized services, online systems of grievance redress, blockchain for procurements, biometric authentication, and real-time dashboards form a technological construct meant to promote transparency, suppress human discretion, and curtail the veil that hangs over transactions in which corruption breeds. But even as technology serves as an agent of disruption to centuries-old rent-seeking systems, it also generates new fields of inequality, exclusion, and monitoring. In this contradiction is the paradox—technology, as with a scalpel, heals or kills, depending on whose fingers hold it and for what end it is used.

In India, pathbreaking initiatives such as Digital India, UIDAI's Aadhaar project, and applications such as Bharat Interface for Money (BHIM) or Government e-Marketplace (GeM) were created to enhance governance to become more efficient and corruption-free. Consider the case of the direct benefit transfer (DBT) model: LPG, pension, or scholarship subsidies are now transferred directly to beneficiaries, bypassing the intermediaries who earlier diverted huge shares. As per the Economic Survey of India (2017-18), these reforms also saved the government more than ₹57,000 crore by doing away with ghost and duplicate beneficiaries. In such a way, technology has proved its transformative capacity—serving as a disinfectant to bring to the surface and erase leakages within the system.

But, as economist and public policy scholar Dr. Reetika Khera has regularly warned, technology can also disenfranchise people it aims to empower. Her rural India fieldwork uncovers how Aadhaar-based authentication failures have resulted in denial of rations and pensions, with marginalized groups like the elderly, illiterate, or physically disabled being the most affected by "technical errors" that are hardly ever accounted for. The systems, while intended to be transparent, do not have adequate grievance mechanisms and enough flexibility for human nuance. Wherever governance is more digitized without proper human scrutiny or social safeguard, it turns impersonal and apathetic.

The issue, therefore, is not technology itself, but technological determinism—the assumption that computers by themselves can change human institutions. Corruption, by definition, is not merely a matter of transactions but of relations, power, and complicity. A corrupt official or politician might no longer receive bribes in the form of cash, but might rig favors in the form of encrypted messages, below-market land acquisitions, or shell corporations—all of which involve investigative nuance beyond most digital systems' ability to detect.

Additionally, technology has produced a new digital elite—those who know how to manipulate algorithms, evade digital oversight, or swamp social media with fabricated stories. The philosopher Byung-Chul Han cautions in his book Psychopolitics that in the digital age, control is not exercised through violence but through seduction, data collection, and willing self-revelation. In such an age, the illusion of transparency can hide deeper manipulations. Citizens are empowered when they can see the status of their passport or file a complaint through an app, but the more significant choices—policy shaping, corporate regulation, or contract allocation—could still occur in unreconstructed boardrooms or behind algorithmic drapes.

Indian political economist Pranab Bardhan correctly points out that development country governance needs a combination of new tools and old accountability frameworks. Village panchayats, school management committees, and ward sabhas, when equipped with information and collective voice, tend to function as more effective checks on corruption than top-down monitoring. Technology should complement, not substitute, these bottom-up participatory frameworks. A biometric system can authenticate identity, but only a watchful community can deliver justice.

There is also the ethical issue of surveillance. Edward Snowden's disclosures regarding global data tracking have demonstrated how governments can utilize technology to monitor citizens in the name of transparency and security. In India, the suggested application of facial recognition technologies and centralized health or education databases is a cause for concern regarding privacy, consent, and authoritarian overreach. As Nandan Nilekani, the mastermind behind Aadhaar, once put it, "Technology must be like plumbing—useful, invisible, and never dictatorial." The risk is that in the quest for clean governance, we might end up building a society that is over-watched so that it cannot breathe freely.

Hence, the imperative of the day is not simply digital literacy but digital democracy. The citizen must not only learn to use an app but know how data gets gathered, stored, used, and sold. The citizen has a right to audit algorithms, question black-box decisions, and hold digital platforms as accountable as any public representative.

In order to de-normalize corruption using technology, it is critical that we create systems that are transparent, inclusive, and participatory. We need to close the digital divide, particularly in rural communities and marginalized sectors. And we cannot confuse automation with reform. A corrupt process automated is still a corrupt process—just quicker and more difficult to track.

In sum, technology is not a savior nor a villain. It is a tool—a potent one—that can either democratize power or centralize it. If harnessed with ethical governance, civic education, and institutional checks, it can light up the dark corners where corruption resides. But left unbridled, it has the potential to become the very architecture that facilitates a new, quiet form of control—one that is less overt, but just as corrosive.

### 5.5 Restoring Trust: Can Ethical Economics Be Done?

As this travel through the anatomy of corruption concludes, we are left with an urgent and uncomfortable question—can we actually envision a world in which economics is guided not only by market reasoning, but by moral reasoning? Can we progress to a world where institutions value equity over expediency, where leaders are guided by integrity without external pressure, and where society does not accept the abnormal as normal? Can trust—so delicate, so frequently broken—ever be rebuilt at scale? Can we, with all our cynicism and exhaustion, still have faith in the concept of ethical economics?

The urge is to respond "no." The evidence of institutional rot is all around us. From electoral funding and crony capitalism to bureaucratic rent-seeking and computer-driven surveillance pretending to be transparency, we exist in an era where economic systems tend to reward the corrupt and penalize the honest. Not only is corruption the norm in this reality—it's also often the unwritten rule. In this reality, the concept of ethical economics itself can appear naive, even farcical. But to give it up is to give way to moral bankruptcy, and in the process of giving way lies the gradual collapse of democracy, justice, and hope.

In order to restore trust, we first need to acknowledge that trust is not a technical variable—it is a moral asset. It cannot be created by apps or legislated by law alone. It has to be earned, demonstrated, and maintained by the ethical behavior of those who exercise power and responsibility. Ethics is not just about staying out of corruption; it is about making fairness, compassion, and sustainability possible at all levels of economic life.

This reality has been reechoed over the centuries. In ancient India, Kautilya (Chanakya) cautioned in the **Arthashastra** that uncontrolled greed within the bureaucracy would corrupt the state from within. Centuries down the line, Mahatma Gandhi underscored that "means are as important as ends," advocating a trusteeship model where the rich are the guardians of social welfare. Now, intellectuals such as Amartya Sen, Jean Drèze, and Ashis Nandy remind us that all development that is missing in moral imagination is bound to increase exclusion and injustice.

Restoring trust will take more than reform. It will take a values revolution. We must redefine success—not merely in terms of GDP but in terms of dignity, environmental balance, and human solidarity. We need a new kind of ethical economists, public officials, business people, and civil society leaders who will not hesitate to utter: the existing system is unjust, and there's a world beyond.

***Can we step toward this vision? Yes—but only if we start to humanize economics once more.***

Think of schools and colleges that educate not just accounting and management but ethics of care, value of truth, and responsibility of power as well. Think of public offices where transparency is not an obligation of compliance but a cultural expectation. Envision markets that reward companies for social investment, not closeness to political centers of power. Envision an internet that enshrines privacy and diffuses knowledge, rather than seeks to manipulate consent and muzzle dissent. Envision a journalism that exposes the corrupt and brings accountability, not journalism that sells silence in a package. Envision a world where honesty is not a rare virtue—but the norm.

***This isn't utopian imagination. This is needed imagination.***

Take the case of New Zealand, where participatory budgeting and well-being indicators inform policy decisions. Or Bhutan, where Gross National Happiness takes precedence over economic growth. Or the emergence of ethical investing, social enterprises, community-owned cooperatives, and public interest litigation—all of which suggest a world crying out for alternatives.

India also has profound wellsprings of moral courage. From the Chipko movement to RTI activists, from whistleblowers within the bureaucracy to grassroots women's self-help groups, there are innumerable instances of courage that reaffirm the ethical heartbeat of the people. What is required is to scale up these ethical actions into structural transformation.

This is the moral economics we need to struggle for. It does not guarantee perfection—it guarantees progress with a conscience. It recognizes human fallibility but demands institutional decency. It allows ambition but balances it with empathy.

To return, then, to our original question—is ethical economics possible? The answer is: it must be. Because the alternative is not just inequality or inefficiency—it is despair. Without ethics, economics becomes a machine that grinds the many for the gain of a few. Without trust, governance becomes performance art and democracy a shell.

***Rebuilding trust is not a matter of policy—it is a matter of principle.***

As this book closes, let us recall that corruption is not inescapable. It is man-made, and what man makes can be undone. But the initial unmaking must be done in the mind—in what we mean by success, by power, and by purpose. Education—actual, humanizing education—possesses the potential for this re-making.

The economy of education is, indeed, an education in economy: one that instills not merely how to gain, but how to value.

For it is as Rabindranath Tagore described, "Where the mind is without fear and the head is held high... into that heaven of freedom, my Father, let my country awake." But that heaven need not be an unattained goal. For we must get there, step by step—as citizens, not as spectators.

The path from corruption to conscience, from fear to fairness, is a long one. But it starts with a decision. And each decision to be ethical is a brick built in the foundation of a more reliable future.

**Let that be our legacy.**

# References

**Books, Papers, and Authors Referenced**

1. **Kautilya (Chanakya).***Arthashastra.* Translations by R. Shamasastry and Patrick Olivelle.

    ○ Used in discussion of bureaucratic corruption and early Indian political economy.

2. **Mahatma Gandhi.***Hind Swaraj* (1909); Collected Works of Mahatma Gandhi.

    ○ Referenced for values on trusteeship, ethical economics, and simplicity.

3. **Amartya Sen.**

    ○ *Development as Freedom* (1999).
    ○ *The Idea of Justice* (2009).
    ○ Used extensively for capability approach, welfare economics, and ethics in governance.

4. **Jean Drèze and Amartya Sen.***An Uncertain Glory: India and its Contradictions* (2013).

    ○ For analysis of institutional shortcomings, social policy, and economic justice.

5. **Ashis Nandy.**

    ○ *The Intimate Enemy* (1983); *Corruption: The Indian Discourse* (1997).
    ○ Referenced for psychological and cultural dimensions of

corruption and power.

6. **Daron Acemoglu and James A. Robinson.***Why Nations Fail* (2012).

   - For institutional design and systemic failure that fosters corruption.

7. **Douglas North.***Institutions, Institutional Change and Economic Performance* (1990).

   - For foundational theories on institutional economics and path dependency.

8. **Robert Klitgaard.***Controlling Corruption* (1988).

   - The formula: Corruption = Monopoly + Discretion – Accountability, used conceptually.

9. **Daniel Kaufmann, Aart Kraay & Massimo Mastruzzi.** World Bank Governance Indicators Reports.

   - Used for empirical support and global corruption patterns.

10. **Joseph Stiglitz.***Globalization and Its Discontents* (2002).

    - For critique of neoliberal policies and the role of elites in shaping corruption.

11. **Thomas Piketty.***Capital in the Twenty-First Century* (2013).

    - Referenced for analysis of inequality, rent-seeking, and class privilege.

12. **Noam Chomsky.**

REFERENCES

- *Media Control* (1991); *Manufacturing Consent* (with Edward S. Herman, 1988).
- Applied in the section on media, manufactured consent, and silence.

13. **Arundhati Roy.**

- *Capitalism: A Ghost Story* (2014).
- For critique of India's corporate-political nexus and co-opted democracy.

14. **Dr. B.R. Ambedkar.**

- *Annihilation of Caste* (1936); *States and Minorities* (1947).
- For foundational ideas on institutional justice and inclusion.

15. **Iris Marion Young.***Justice and the Politics of Difference* (1990).

- Cited for perspectives on structural injustice and marginalization.

16. **John Rawls.***A Theory of Justice* (1971).

- For the principles of fairness and institutional morality.

17. **Gunnar Myrdal.***Asian Drama: An Inquiry into the Poverty of Nations* (1968).

- Used in contextualizing systemic inequality and bureaucratic inertia in South Asia.

18. **Rajni Kothari.***Politics in India* (1970); and journal articles.

- Referenced for patronage politics, corruption, and democratic degeneration.

19. **Partha Chatterjee.**_The Politics of the Governed_ (2004).

   - For postcolonial perspectives on state-society relations and micro-politics.

20. **Ha-Joon Chang.**_Kicking Away the Ladder_ (2002).

   - Referenced to critique neoliberal prescriptions and developmental double standards.

21. **Prabhat Patnaik.**

   - Various writings in _People's Democracy_ and _Economic and Political Weekly_.
   - For Marxist critique of capitalist collusion and state complicity.

22. **Yogendra Yadav.**

   - Public writings and election studies used in analyzing electoral funding and moral disengagement.

23. **Vinay Lal.**_The History of History_ (2003); lectures on colonial knowledge systems and ethics.

   - Referenced in cultural and ethical framing of Indian political economy.

24. **Transparency International.**_Corruption Perceptions Index (annual reports)._

   - Used for global ranking and perception-based metrics of corruption.

25. **UNDP Human Development Reports.**

- ◦ Especially for linking education, governance, and sustainable development.

26. **World Economic Forum and World Bank Reports.**

   - ◦ For data on trust erosion, state capacity, and institutional integrity.

27. **RTI Activist Case Studies and Public Interest Litigations in India.**

   - ◦ For demonstrating grassroots movements against institutional corruption.

28. **Bhagavad Gita and Dhammapada.**

   - ◦ Referenced in philosophical reflections on duty, desire, and detachment in ethical contexts.

29. **Rabindranath Tagore.**

   - ◦ *Gitanjali*, especially the poem "Where the mind is without fear".
   - ◦ Used as a closing spiritual and aspirational message of ethical awakening.